CULTURES OF THE WORLD
Lithuania

Cavendish
Square
New York

Published in 2018 by Cavendish Square Publishing, LLC
243 5th Avenue, Suite 136, New York, NY 10016
Copyright © 2018 by Cavendish Square Publishing, LLC

Third Edition

Library of Congress Cataloging-in-Publication Data

Names: Kagda, Sakina, 1939- author. | Latif, Zawiah Abdul, author. | Nevins,
   Debbie, author.
Title: Lithuania / Sakina Kagda, Zawiah Abdul Latif, Debbie Nevins.
Other titles: Lithuania (Cavendish Square Publishing)
Description: New York : Cavendish Square Publishing, 2018. | Series: Cultures
   of the world | Includes bibliographical references and index.
Identifiers: LCCN 2017000419 (print) | LCCN 2017000890 (ebook) | ISBN
   9781502627391 (library bound) | ISBN 9781502627346 (E-book)
Subjects: LCSH: Lithuania--Juvenile literature.
Classification: LCC DK505.23 .K34 2018 (print) | LCC DK505.23 (ebook) | DDC
   947.93--dc23

Writers, Sakina Kagda, Zawiah Abdul Latif; Debbie Nevins, third edition
Editorial Director, third edition: David McNamara
Editor, third edition: Debbie Nevins
Art Director, third edition: Amy Greenan
Designer, third edition: Jessica Nevins
Picture Researcher, third edition: Jessica Nevins

PICTURE CREDITS

PRECEDING PAGE
Two little sisters wave Lithuanian flags in Vilnius.

Printed in the United States of America

CONTENTS

LITHUANIA TODAY

BANDS PLAYED, FIREWORKS DAZZLED, AND CROWDS CHEERED
on May 1, 2004, the day Lithuania became a part of the European Union (EU).
The celebration in Vilnius, Lithuania's capital city, reflected the optimism of
a new era. In the city center, banners proclaimed Bukime Europieciais! ("Let's be
Europeans!") and Mes Europoje! ("We are in Europe!")

Of course, Lithuania has always been in Europe. In fact, it's the geographical
center of the continent, so its inclusion has never been in doubt. Not only that, but
centuries ago, it was the one of the largest and most powerful countries in Europe.
So why the fuss?

The EU is a political and economic union of twenty-eight European countries
(as of 2016), and on that day in 2004, Lithuania and nine other countries became
new members. Three of them, the Baltic states of Lithuania, Estonia, and Latvia, had
once been part of the Soviet Union (USSR)—the massive Union of Soviet Socialist
Republics that stretched from Europe to Asia from 1922 to 1991. The Soviet giant
was dominated by Russia, the huge country at its core. In 1940, the Soviets annexed
Lithuania and its Baltic neighbors, only to have those territories invaded and occupied

EURAS – LIETUVOS VALIUTA
NUO 2015 M. SAUSIO 1 D.

A digital clock above the entrance to the Bank of Lithuania counts the time until the country adopts the euro on January 1, 2015.

by Nazi Germany in 1941. In 1944, the reluctant and essentially powerless Baltic states were taken over once again by the Soviets—and subjected to the terror of Joseph Stalin, the brutal Soviet leader until his death in 1953.

As part of the Soviet Union, Lithuania learned to look to the East for its cultural identity and to communism for its political leadership. Generations of Lithuanians were indoctrinated in the Soviet way of life, but for the most part, they remained distrustful of the regime. As the Soviet Union began to crumble in the 1980s, independence-minded Lithuanians pushed for freedom. In 1991, they succeeded. Lithuania has been its own nation since that time. Unshackled from the behemoth that was Russia and its satellites, the country is now able to establish its own identity. For that, it has turned its head and now looks West, to Europe.

Joining the EU, therefore, symbolized an enormous shift in the way Lithuania sees itself. A few months after becoming members of the EU, Lithuania and its Baltic neighbors also joined NATO, the North Atlantic Treaty Organization. NATO is a military alliance for the purpose of mutual defense, made up of twenty-six European nations, the United States, and Canada.

Tellingly, one of the founding goals of NATO in 1949 was a defense against Soviet invasion. An updated concern, certainly for Lithuania, is now one of Russian invasion. In the wake of Russian intervention in Ukraine in 2014, the concern may be well-founded.

In November 2016, eleven NATO countries sent four thousand troops to Lithuania to participate in training exercises near the Russian border. That's more than twice the number

Lithuanian soldiers prepare to march in a parade in Vilnius during the Iron Sword military exercises in 2016.

previously employed in years past. Lithuania itself contributed its newly-formed Žemaitija (Iron Wolf) brigade, made up of soldiers conscripted after the country reinstated mandatory military service in 2015. This is just one of the many ways in which Lithuania and the other Baltic states are trying to keep Moscow at bay.

In the life of a nation, twenty-some years—the period since Lithuania's independence in 1991—is not a long time. Lithuania today is still recreating itself, reaching back to its pre-Soviet heritage as it looks ahead to the future. It's not an easy task. Undergoing rapid de-Sovietization in favor of Europeanization—not only of its economic and political structures, but also in the hearts and minds of its people—has involved tremendous change. Great change, even for the better, often creates great uncertainty, which can breed instability and fear.

Transitioning from a state-run, communist economy to a largely private, free-market economy has been an enormous challenge for Lithuania, but so far, the country has managed it quite well. Joining the EU and the eurozone helped significantly to stabilize the process. The 2016 Index of Economic Freedom ranked Lithuania a very high number 13 out of 186 countries. The index, an annual guide published by The Heritage Foundation and The Wall

Street Journal, measures and evaluates national economies based on its definition of "economic freedom," which reportedly correlates with prosperity. Indeed, Lithuania is one of the fastest growing economies in the EU.

There are other indications of Lithuania's success in the twenty-first century as well. The numbers of people pursuing higher education have steadily risen so that Lithuania now has a higher percentage of students than any other EU country. Salaries more than doubled between 1998 and 2008, yet they remain among the lowest in the EU.

Tourism to the country is on the increase. In 2013, some 1.2 million people visited Lithuania, an increase of 10.5 percent over the year before. Most visitors come from neighboring countries, with German tourists topping the list in 2015. Among its attractions, Lithuania boasts three UNESCO World Heritage sites. The United Nations Educational, Scientific, and Cultural Organization (UNESCO) World Heritage Center identifies sites of cultural and natural heritage all over the world that it considers to be of "outstanding

People walk along Pilies Street in the Old Town section of Vilnius, a popular route with numerous attractive shops.

A panoramic view of Old Town, Vilnius.

universal value to humanity." One of those sites is the Curonian Spit, a nearly 61-mile-long (98 km) thin, curved, sand-dune spit that separates the Curonian Lagoon from the Baltic Sea on its southwestern coast. Lithuania also has seaside resorts, spa towns, national parks, and pilgrimage sites, such as the Hill of Crosses in the town of Samogitia. Above all, it has Vilnius, its capital city and top attraction, with its Baroque architecture and rich cultural offerings. Within it lies the Old Town, one of the largest surviving medieval towns in Northern Europe, and itself another World Heritage Site.

Will Lithuania's turn toward Europe and away from Russia continue to work to its advantage? Or will Europe's own problems, and specifically those of the EU itself, put stumbling blocks in the way? Will Russia's desire for more access to the Baltic Sea prove a threat to the three former Soviet countries that lie in its way? The future is, as always, uncertain, but Lithuania is posed to tackle it with vigor and optimism.

GEOGRAPHY

Storks stand in a large treetop nest in Bitenai, Lithuania.

1

LITHUANIA IS ONE OF THREE countries, along with Estonia and Latvia, commonly known as the Baltic States. These northern European nations are located on the eastern coast of the Baltic Sea. For much of the twentieth century, they were among the republics that made up the Soviet Union—the Union of Soviet Socialist Republics (USSR). This trio share a similar topography as well as many common cultural elements. Lithuania is the largest and most populous of the three.

Lithuania covers 25,174 square miles (65,200 square km), just a bit larger than the state of West Virginia. Its surface area is about the size of Denmark or Ireland.

Geographically, Lithuania stands at the very heart of Europe. In 1989, the French National Geographic Institute certified that the exact geographical center of Europe is located in the town of Purnuskes, 17 miles (27 km) north of the Lithuanian capital, Vilnius. Lithuania's neighbors are Latvia in the north, Belarus in the east and south, and Poland and the Kaliningrad Oblast region of the Russian Federation in the southwest. On the west it borders the Baltic Sea.

Lithuania is known as the land of storks. The *gandras*, or white stork, was named the national bird in 1973. The country hosts about thirteen thousand nesting pairs, according to a 2004-2005 international white stork census. Lithuanians believe storks bring harmony to the families on whose property they nest. According to folklore, storks also bring babies.

A small lake reflects the wide sky in a flat region of farmland and trees in Lithuania.

PHYSICAL GEOGRAPHY

The Baltic states are characterized by flat farmlands alternating with low rolling hills formed during the last ice age. Many small rivers, lakes, and scattered pine forests add personality to the landscape. The plains sometimes sink into large tracts of swampland. The region is dotted with ancient city centers ringed with Soviet-era concrete housing projects.

Lithuania can be roughly divided into four ethnographic regions:

AUKŠTAITIJA ("highland" in Lithuanian) in the east is characterized by gently rolling hills, pine forests, and hundreds of lakes.

ŽEMAITIJA is a moderately high area in the northwest and is traditionally noted for its dialect, roadside shrines, and local dress.

SUVALKIJA in the south is to the west of the Nemunas River, and

DZŪKIJA is a hilly southern region east of the Nemunas River.

Other main landscape regions include:

THE CENTRAL LOWLANDS is the region in northern Lithuania between Aukštaitija and Žemaitija. This flat land is largely agricultural, although the cities of Šiauliai, Joniškis, and Panevėžys are heavily industrialized.

THE BALTIC SEACOAST is marked by sandy beaches and magnificent dunes.

THE KAUNAS REGION is generally flat and agricultural except for the steep hills bordering the Nemunas River valley.

THE VILNIUS REGION is a hilly area with many farms as well as the capital and its surrounding multicultural district. Lithuania's highest point, a 963-foot (294-m) hill called Juozapinė, is located in this area.

CLIMATE

The climate in Lithuania is a mixture of maritime and continental. In the coastal zone, the climate is maritime. In the eastern part of the country, it is continental. The mean annual temperature is about 43°F (6°C) with an average temperature in July of 63°F (17°C). There are four distinct seasons. In spring the weather is warm and the land is full of blossoms. Summers have moderate heat, adequate humidity, and a sufficient number of sunny days for vegetation growth. Fall and winter are cold and long.

The mean annual rainfall varies from 21 inches (53 cm) in the central lowlands to 37 inches (94 cm) on the southwestern slopes of the Žemaitija hills. The greatest amount of rain falls in August at the seaside. The growing season is relatively short, varying between 169 and 202 days.

RIVERS, LAKES, AND WOODLANDS

Lithuania is a land of notable scenic beauty, with meandering rivers, thousands of lakes, and ancient woodlands rich in wildlife. Forests, including pine, spruce, birch, black alder, aspen, oak, and ash, cover about 32 percent of the total land area. Large tracts of land are bogs and marshland.

Lithuania has a large, dense river network. The waters of the Minija, Musa, Venta, Jura, Sesupe, Dubysa, and Nemunas rivers flow through the country. There are 816 rivers longer than 6 miles (10 km), most of them tributaries of the Nemunas, which flows for 582 miles (937 km). Of this, 295 miles (475 km) is within Lithuania's borders.

Lithuanians like to refer to their country as Nemunasland, due to the great love they have for their river Nemunas. In pre-Christian times, waters and forests were considered to be sacred.

There are about 2,830 lakes with a total area of about 340 square miles (880 square km), making up 1.5 percent of the country's total territory. The largest man-made freshwater lake is the Kaunas Reservoir (Kauno Marios), also called the Curonian Lagoon, a dammed body of water east of Kaunas. The Kaunas Reservoir has an area of 24.5 square miles (63.5 square km). The dam has turned this part of the Nemunas River into a recreational area, and pleasure boats still make the journey from the Kaunas to the Baltic Sea. The deepest lake, Tauragnas, is 200 feet (61 m) deep. Most of the lakes are concentrated in the Aukštaitija hills around Ignalina.

NATIONAL PARKS

The Soviet years contributed to the preservation of nature in Lithuania, ironically, because of Moscow's heavy-handed mismanagement of the country. The percentage of unused land increased after 1940 as the rural population migrated to other countries or was deported to Siberia. As farmlands decreased, forests took over the abandoned land.

Lithuania therefore retains large tracts of beaches, woodlands, and wilderness that have vanished elsewhere in Europe because of overdevelopment. Vast reserves of Lithuania's wilderness are protected by its five national parks. The first, Aukštaitija National Park, was designated in 1974 and covers an area of 100,251 acres (40,572 hectares). Over 70 percent of this park is pine forest. Its beautiful lakes and rivers attract tourists, naturalists, and ethnographers, who study the many ancient buildings and villages in the park.

Dzukija National Park was established to preserve the old villages, the historical and cultural monuments, and the beautiful forests of southeastern Lithuania. Eighty-five percent of the park is covered by woods.

One of the serene lakes in Aukštaitija National Park.

On the Baltic coast is Kursiu Marios (Curonian Lagoon), Lithuania's largest inland body of water. A narrow strip of land called the Kursiu Nerija (Curonian Spit) separates Kursiu Marios from the Baltic Sea. Kursiu Nerija National Park is located on this spit. Until the fifteenth century the area was covered with forest, but as a result of heavy logging the sand cover was nearly destroyed, and shifting sand dunes sometimes covered whole villages. Attempts to reforest the area to stabilize the dunes have been successful. Today, about 17,297 acres (7,000 ha) of forests protect life on the spit. The other national parks are at Trakai and Žemaitija.

A WILDLIFE PARADISE

Because of its large areas of forest and marsh, Lithuania is home to a variety of animals and birds. Ducks, waders, terns, and swans can be found in the coastal wetlands, while birds of prey, corncrakes, and white storks inhabit the uplands, and hooded crows haunt the cities. The forests and rivers have elk, deer, marten, lynx, boars, beavers, and otters. Occasionally, even brown bears can be spotted in the brush.

Trophy hunting is popular with sportsmen from other European countries, such as the Germans who visit Lithuania to hunt wolves. Wild game felled by professional hunters has always been popular on Lithuanian menus, but recreational hunting has not been a common pastime in the Baltic states.

Lithuania's largest cities are Vilnius (population 535,216 in 2013,), Kaunas (308,831), Klaipeda (159,342), Siauliai (107,080), and Panevėžys (98,598 in 2016).

The Neris River wends through the capital city of Vilnius.

VILNIUS Lithuania's capital, Vilnius, is one of the major industrial, scientific, and cultural centers of the Baltic region. The city was founded in 1323 by Grand Duke Gediminas. After dreaming of an iron wolf howling from a hill near the Vilnia River, he invited merchants and craftsmen to settle on the site and build a city. By the sixteenth century, Vilnius had become one of the major cities of Europe. Vilnius University, founded in 1579, is one of the oldest institutions of higher learning in Europe.

The numerous churches that characterize Vilnius were impounded for other uses during the Soviet years, but are now being restored and resanctified. The city's first church, the cathedral, was built in 1387. Rebuilt repeatedly over the centuries, it was the first church to be reconstructed following independence.

KAUNAS Kaunas is Lithuania's second-largest city. Its rivalry with Vilnius dates to 1920, when it became the provisional capital after Vilnius was occupied by Poland. Today it is the major commercial center of the country. Kaunas is the most Lithuanian of all the country's cities. More than 93 percent of its population is ethnic Lithuanian, and much of the old city has survived both World War II and the Soviet period.

TRAKAI

Trakai was the capital of the Grand Duchy during the Middle Ages. Today it is a popular resort village in a beautiful region of lakes, forests, and hills west of Vilnius. The heart of Trakai is its castle, probably built by Grand Duke Jaunutis (Gediminas's son) between 1362 and 1382. The complex of defensive fortifications and castle stands on both a peninsula and an island. It is the only island castle still standing in northeastern Europe. The castle is now impressively restored and stands as a monument to the past glory of the medieval Lithuanian state.

The town of Trakai consists mainly of old wooden buildings along with a few modern ones. It is the home of the Karaites, a tribe of Turks brought to Lithuania in the late fourteenth century by Grand Duke Vytautas to serve as his bodyguards.

INTERNET LINKS

https://www.lonelyplanet.com/lithuania
This travel site offers beautiful pictures and information about Lithuania's cities and regions.

http://www.mapsofworld.com/lithuania/lithuania-river-map.html
Maps of the World offers a map of Lithuania's rivers, as well as maps of its cities, roads, and more.

http://www.visitlithuania.net/nature
This tourism site provides wide-ranging information and photos relating to nature in Lithuania, including its rivers, lakes, national parks, and wildlife.

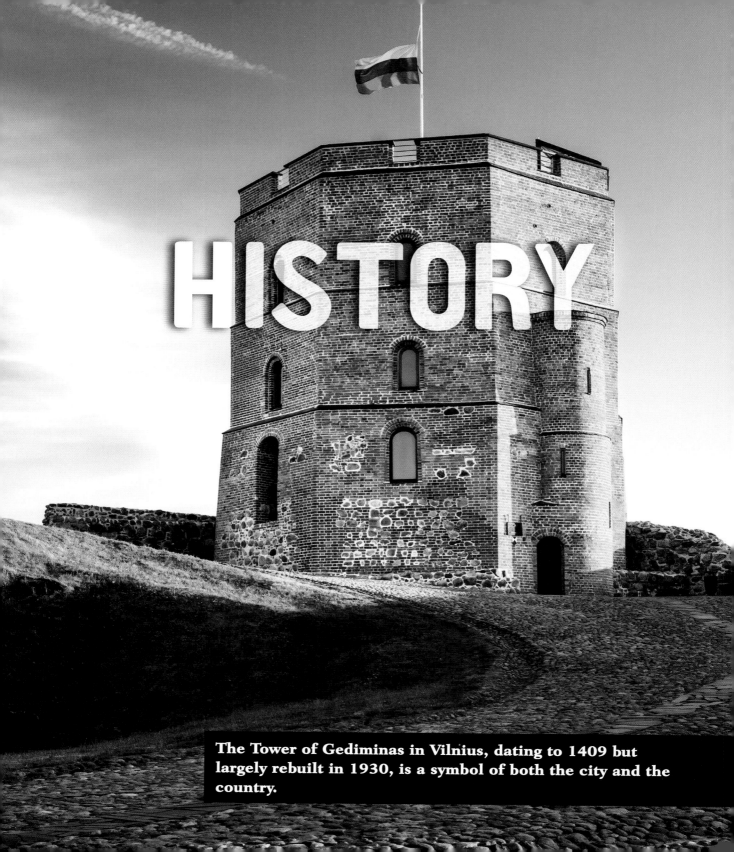

HISTORY

The Tower of Gediminas in Vilnius, dating to 1409 but largely rebuilt in 1930, is a symbol of both the city and the country.

2

AS AN INDEPENDENT NATION, Lithuania's history is not long. And yet, as a region, a culture, and a people, its history extends far back in time. As Lithuanians grapple with the economic and political growing pains of their newly-independent country, they look back for inspiration to the time when the Grand Duchy of Lithuania was one of the largest countries in Europe, stretching from the Baltic Sea in the north to the Black Sea in the south, and from Poland in the west nearly to Moscow in the east. More recently, they can recall the tranquil period between the two world wars when Lithuania was an independent and successful nation.

Those periods of greatness have, however, been overshadowed in Lithuania's history by centuries of domination by its powerful neighbors—Poland, Russia, Germany, and Sweden, each of which has vied for control of this strategically important territory. During these long periods of domination, Lithuanians struggled to maintain their separate

The first time the name Lithuania occurs in written text is in the Quedlinburg Annals, a history of the Holy Roman Empire, written in 1009 at the convent of Quedlinburg Abbey in Germany. The passage relates the killing that year of the archbishop St. Bruno and eighteen of his followers by "pagans" "at the Rus and Lithuanian border."

identity and culture. They have preserved their language, their religion, and their traditions in spite of repeated intrusive attempts to obliterate all traces of ancient Lithuania.

THE EARLY LITHUANIANS

The prehistoric inhabitants of the Baltic region were nomadic hunters and, at a later time, farmers. Around 2500 BCE, Indo-European tribes spread across the region that is now western Russia, Ukraine, Belarus, and Poland, eventually concentrating along the Baltic shoreline. They merged with the indigenous population and formed a number of distinct tribes in the territory that is now Lithuania. At the end of the first century CE, the Roman historian Tacitus described the people living around the Baltic Sea in his history of Germany. He noted that they traded in amber and that they were able farmers, saying that in the growing of crops they worked "with more patience than is customary among the lazy Germans."

From the second to the fifth century, the Baltic tribes enjoyed a golden age in which they developed a trading empire that webbed northeastern Europe. During the ninth and tenth centuries, Vikings from Scandinavia launched raids on the prosperous coastal regions of the Baltic, and the Baltic tribes and the Vikings alternately fought and traded with each other.

The tenth century also saw the start of feudalism in the Baltic region and the emergence of the Lithuanians—the largest tribe—as dominant on Lithuanian territory. Naturally barricaded by impenetrable forests and thousands of lakes, Lithuania remained largely isolated until the fourteenth century.

THE GRAND DUCHY

During the thirteenth century, German crusaders invaded the Baltic region in a bid to conquer and Christianize the last remaining pagan tribes in Europe. The Knights of the Sword and their successors, the Teutonic Knights, overpowered the tribes of Latvia and Estonia, creating the country of Livonia.

As the other Baltic tribes fell to the German knights, only the Lithuanians succeeded in maintaining their independence. In 1236 the Lithuanian grand duke Mindaugas unified the small feudal states of the region into a duchy, a territory ruled by a duke or duchess. The united Lithuania struck a powerful blow against the Knights of the Sword at Siauliai.

The formation of the state was completed by the grand dukes Traidenis (who reigned 1270–1282) and Vytenis (1295–1316). Vytenis left a large state with clearly defined policies to his brother Gediminas (1316–1341). Under Gediminas, the Lithuanian territory was expanded as far as Kiev and the Black Sea.

This map shows the approximate areas where various Baltic tribes lived around the time of Mindaugas.

ALLIANCE WITH POLAND

The Lithuanian leaders were successful in resisting the ongoing attacks by the Teutonic Knights, but under increased pressure in the late fourteenth century, they decided to ally themselves with Poland, which was also fighting the crusaders. In 1385 Lithuanian nobles arranged the marriage of Grand Duke Jogaila of Lithuania to Princess Jadwiga of Poland. The match was quite advantageous—Jadwiga's husband would become king of Poland—but there were strings attached: Jogaila must become a Christian and convert his whole empire as well. Jogaila agreed, was baptized as Ladislaus, and assumed the crowns of Poland and Lithuania. Lithuania was the last European country to adopt Christianity.

Mindaugas (c. 1203–1263) was Lithuania's first and only king. All other monarchs which came later were rulers of both Poland and Lithuania combined, but today Mindaugas is celebrated as the nation's founder. Not that much is known about him. He probably inherited his dukedom—by the age of sixteen or so, he was considered an "elder duke"—and, along with other dukes, presided over various fiefdoms and tribes that populated the region in the thirteenth century. He rose to power through military conquests and a string of political marriages, and is credited with uniting the Baltic people into the Grand Duchy of Lithuania. By 1236, he was said to be the leader of all Lithuanians.

In 1251 Mindaugas adopted the Catholic faith in order to protect his country from becoming a target of the crusading knights. He was coronated in 1253 by Pope Innocent IV, temporarily making Lithuania part of the Holy Roman Empire. The Lithuanian king's Christianity was probably only political and not spiritual, and he renounced the faith after about ten years. His religious conversion had not brought him the kind of political gains that he had hoped. Meanwhile, other Lithuanian dukes were irked by his actions, figuring they had as much claim to ruling Lithuania as Mindaugas had, and were unhappy with being governed by the Holy Roman Emperor and the pope. Despite the king's conversion to Christianity, most Lithuanians remained pagans.

Mindaugas was assassinated in 1263, after taking the wife of a Lithuanian duke. Reportedly, two of the king's sons were also murdered at that time. Although history is hazy on whether other sons survived, Mindaugas did not leave a dynasty of heirs, and his family's connections with ruling Lithuania end with him. After his death, Lithuania reverted to being a pagan nation.

Mindaugas was more or less forgotten until the nineteenth century, when a wave of Lithuanian nationalism revived his reputation. In 1990, the Lithuanian government declared July 6, the day of the coronation of King Mindaugas, to be a public holiday, also known as Statehood Day. The 750th anniversary of his coronation was marked in 2003 by the dedication of the Mindaugas Bridge in Vilnius.

After the marriage of Jogaila and Jadwiga, Polish feudal lords tried to abolish the Grand Duchy of Lithuania, but their efforts were resisted by the Lithuanian aristocracy, and Lithuania maintained its separate identity. Jogaila's reign in Poland (1386—1434) started the long period of a Lithuanian-Polish common history, which survived until the eighteenth century.

VYTAUTAS THE GREAT

After Jogaila, the position of grand duke of Lithuania was given to his cousin Vytautas, who became the last of the great Lithuanian rulers. He drove back the Turks, and under his rule, which flourished from the late fourteenth to the early fifteenth centuries, the grand duchy became one of the largest states in Europe.

The Teutonic Knights continued their attempts to conquer Lithuania. Finally, in 1410, the Lithuanians and the Poles defeated them at the Battle of Tannenberg, ending the Knights' ambitions in the Baltic.

Poland put its cultural stamp on Lithuania. The Lithuanian nobility were quick to appreciate that they would gain personally from Poland's rigid and efficient social and political order. The pre-Christian religion vanished as Roman Catholicism took hold. The nobility spoke Latin at court and Polish elsewhere.

In 1569, weakened by frequent fights with Russia, Lithuania joined with Poland to form the Union of Lublin, "a commonwealth of two nations." Lithuania retained its territory, legislation, treasury, and army, but shared Poland's king and government. The merger did not help strengthen Lithuania, though, and the grand duchy slowly declined.

The Lithuanian Grand Duke Vytautas is shown in a fragment of a painting of the Battle of Gunvald by the nineteenth-century Polish artist Jan Matejko.

THE VYTIS

The state emblem of the Republic of Lithuania is the Vytis (VEE-tis), the White Knight. It shows a white knight in armor on a white horse, holding a raised sword in his right hand. A blue shield on the left shoulder of the knight has a gold double cross.

The charging knight was first used as the state emblem in 1366 on the seal of Grand Duke Algirdas. With minor stylistic changes, the Vytis remained the state emblem of the Grand Duchy of Lithuania until the eighteenth century. When Lithuania was annexed by the Russian Empire in 1795, the Vytis was incorporated into the imperial state emblem.

In time, the charging knight came to stand for a patriotic knight chasing an intruder out of his country. Banned under Soviet rule, the Vytis became an enduring symbol of the Lithuanian drive for independence.

RUSSIAN OCCUPATION

The disintegration of the grand duchy in the eighteenth century led to an economic, social, and political crisis exacerbated by wars with Sweden, Russia, and Turkey. Lithuania was partitioned three times (in 1772, 1793, 1795), with different countries claiming parts of it. In 1795 Lithuania was absorbed by the Russian Empire, except for a small part that was incorporated into Prussia.

In reaction to peasant uprisings, Russia began an intensive process of Russification. The goal was to eradicate all traces of ancient Lithuania. Landholding rights were limited to followers of the Russian Orthodox religion. Vilnius University was shut down in 1832, and only Russians were admitted to schools above the elementary level. Starting in 1864, the Lithuanian language and the Latin alphabet in which it was written were banned.

Although Lithuanians tried to resist the Russian occupation, their uprisings in 1831 and 1863 failed. In their wake, Russification became more intense, but resistance continued. For example, Lithuanian-language books were printed in the Prussian portion of Lithuania and secretly smuggled into Lithuania, where they were quietly circulated. In 1883, the first Lithuanian newspaper, *Ausra*, was published. When that was brutally crushed, *Varpas* sprang up. From 1891 to 1893, the Russian border police confiscated 37,718 Lithuanian books and newspapers. From 1900 to 1902, they seized 56,182 publications. The ban on the press was finally lifted in 1904.

PROCLAMATION OF AN INDEPENDENT STATE

Popular demands for Lithuanian autonomy continued to surface. When World War I turned Lithuania into a battlefield, in the fall of 1915, its entire territory was occupied by Germans, who had already defeated the Russians. Resistance continued to mount, though, and on February 16, 1918, Lithuania proclaimed its independence. Germany recognized the new state in 1918 as did Russia in 1920.

Nonetheless, Lithuania continued to face problems with its neighbors. In October 1920 Poland occupied Vilnius, causing the capital to be transferred to Kaunas. In 1921 the duchy was admitted to the League of Nations. A democratic constitution was adopted in 1922, and the litas became the currency.

Nationalist Party leader Antanas Smetona became Lithuania's first president. He served as president from 1919 to 1920, and then again became president in late 1926 after seizing power in a military coup. One year later, in 1927, he dismissed parliament and became the authoritarian leader of Lithuania until 1940.

A copy of the Aušra ("Dawn") newspaper, published in 1884.

On August 23, 1989, some two million people—about half of them Lithuanians—joined hands to form a human chain spanning about 420 miles (675.5 kilometers) across the three Baltic states. The chain extended from Vilnius, Lithuania, to Riga, Latvia, to Tallinn, Estonia, connecting the three capitals. Video footage taken from planes and helicopters show

an almost continuous line of people across the countryside.

The "Baltic Way" demonstrators peacefully linked hands for fifteen minutes at 7 pm local time. In addition, a number of local gatherings and protests took place. Priests held masses or rang church bells. In Vilnius, about five thousand people gathered afterwards in the Cathedral Square, holding candles and singing patriotic songs.

The date of the demonstration was significant. It marked the fiftieth anniversary of the Molotov–Ribbentrop Pact, a 1939 nonaggression treaty between the Soviet Union and Nazi Germany. The agreement contained secret protocols that, along with subsequent secret agreements, divided Europe into German and Soviet spheres of influence and cleared the way for the Soviet occupation and annexation of the Baltics in 1940.

The event, organised by Baltic pro-independence movements, including the Sąjūdis of Lithuania, was designed to attract international attention to the Baltic people's desire for independence. It also illustrated solidarity among the three nations. The Soviet authorities in Moscow called the demonstration "nationalist hysteria." but failed to do anything about it. Within seven months, Lithuania became the first of the Soviet republics to declare independence.

The Baltic Way protest was one of the earliest and longest unbroken human chains in history. Documents recording the event were added to UNESCO's Memory of the World Register in 2009.

During these twenty-two years of independence before the Soviets overran the country, Lithuania's economy grew to compete with those of Western European countries. Lithuanians later looked back on that time with nostalgia, and they longed to return to it all through the fifty hard years that followed as a Soviet republic.

SOVIET AND GERMAN OCCUPATIONS

On June 14, 1940, the Soviet Union issued an ultimatum to Lithuania, demanding the resignation of its government. It had to yield, and on the night of July 11, 1940, more than two thousand people were deported, including members of the government who hadn't simply been executed, and a new pro-Soviet government was installed. Within a few days, Lithuania was incorporated into the Soviet Union. The incorporation was not recognized as legal by any Western government. In June of 1941, another thirty-four thousand Lithuanians were deported to Siberia.

In Vilnius, in 2011, people place flowers on a cattle wagon used in the Soviet deportation of Lithuanians to Siberia, to mark the seventieth anniversary of the terrible event.

The Russian occupation was overcome by the German army, which occupied Lithuania from 1941 until 1944. During that time, the Nazis executed about 175,000 Lithuanian Jews and 16,000 ethnic Lithuanians, and deported another 36,000 Lithuanians to labor and concentration camps in Germany. The large Jewish community in Vilnius was almost entirely wiped out.

In 1944 the Soviet Union once again took Lithuania under the umbrella of its Communist regime. There were mass deportations, in which the Soviets sent more than 350,000 Lithuanians to labor camps in Siberia. Many of those deported died along the way. Farms were reorganized into a collective farm program, and the Lithuanian economy became subordinated to the demands of the greater Soviet economy. Religion was suppressed, as were other aspects of Lithuanian culture. Many ordinary freedoms were eliminated.

By the late 1980s the Soviet economy was in a desperate condition. The Soviet leader, Mikhail Gorbachev, introduced the reform policies of *glasnost* (openness) and *perestroika* (restructuring). Under these new policies, Soviet citizens were encouraged to voice their opinions and to participate in the reform of the Soviet system. This new openness led to the clamorous emergence of independence movements in many of the Soviet republics. One of these was Lithuania.

INDEPENDENCE AT LAST

On February 7, 1990, the Lithuanian Communist Party proclaimed the 1944 Soviet annexation to have been illegal. It was supported by Sąjudis,

Protestors rally for freedom and independence on the eve of Soviet leader Mikhail Gorbachev's visit to the rebellious Lithuanian republic in January 1990.

a proindependence party. In national elections held in 1990, Sąjudis won a majority in the parliament. By the Act of March 11, 1990, the Lithuanian parliament declared the restoration of the independence of the Republic of Lithuania. Vytautas Landsbergis, the new leader of parliament, formed a cabinet of ministers under Prime Minister Kazimiera Prunskiene, and adopted a constitution. The Soviet government announced an economic embargo and sent tanks to Vilnius, but faced with vociferous international disapproval, they agreed to negotiate.

Little progress was made in the negotiations, and on January 13, 1991, Soviet tank units seized radio and television stations. Fourteen Lithuanians were killed in the confrontation. In August of 1991, an attempted coup of the Soviet government failed in Moscow, and Lithuania's independence was recognized internationally soon afterward. Lithuania was admitted to the United Nations in September 1991 and joined the Council of Europe the following year. In June of 1993, the litas was reintroduced as the national currency.

In 2004, Lithuania joined the North Atlantic Treaty Organization (NATO) and the European Union (EU), and in 2008, the Lithuanian parliament banned the display of Soviet and Nazi symbols. In January 2015, Lithuania joined the Eurozone, and adopted the euro (EUR) as the national currency.

INTERNET LINKS

http://www.bbc.com/news/world-europe-17540745
BBC News presents a timeline of key events in Lithuanian history from 1915 to 2012.

http://www.thebalticway.eu/en
The Baltic Way site presents a map, timeline, personal stories, and other information about the historic "human chain" event.

http://www.truelithuania.com/topics/history-and-politics-of-lithuania/history-of-lithuania
This site gives in-depth but concise coverage of Lithuanian history.

GOVERNMENT

The Lithuanian flag waves on Independence Day, February 16, 2016, in Vilnius.

3

THE REPUBLIC OF LITHUANIA IS AN independent democratic nation. The foundations of its political and social system are stipulated in the constitution, which was adopted in October 1992. The constitution declares that state power in Lithuania is "exercised by the Seimas [parliament], the President, the Government, and the Judiciary."

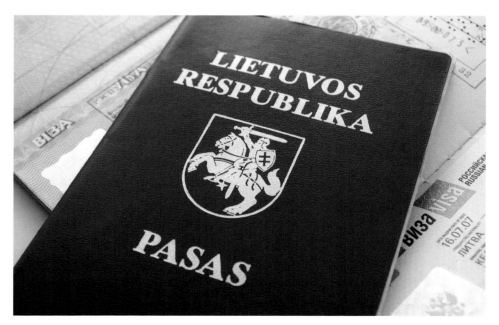

A Lithuanian passport is emblazoned with the national emblem of the Vytis, the White Knight.

Unlike in the United States and many other nations, Lithuanian citizenship is attained by descent rather than by birth. A child born in Lithuania is not automatically a citizen of that country, but is only granted citizenship if at least one parent is a Lithuanian citizen.

THE CONSTITUTION

On May 18, 1989, the Lithuanian Supreme Soviet—the highest legislative body in Soviet Lithuania—adopted a declaration of Lithuanian sovereignty that asserted the supremacy of Lithuania's laws over those from Moscow. A general election in February and March 1990 resulted in a pro-independence majority in the Supreme Soviet, and that body affirmed the restoration of Lithuanian independence. The Lithuanian Supreme Soviet was renamed the Supreme Council. It brought back the pre-1940 name of the country (the Republic of Lithuania) and adopted the Provisional Fundamental Law of the Republic of Lithuania, which restored portions of the Lithuanian constitution of 1938. It established the rights, freedoms, and duties of the country's citizens.

A new constitution was approved in a national referendum in October 1992. It created a strong presidential system with a legislature of 141 elected representatives and a Council of Ministers headed by a prime minister.

LEGISLATIVE BRANCH

The parliament is the Seimas (SAY-mahs), formerly called the Supreme Council. About half of the 141 members of this legislative body are elected in individual constituencies and the other half are elected by nationwide vote according to proportional representation. With the approval of the Seimas, the president of Lithuania appoints the Council of Ministers, which is the highest authority of executive power. The Council of Ministers is headed by the prime minister.

As the highest state authority, the Seimas has the power to adopt laws, consider proposals of programs produced by the government, approve the budget of the government, establish the state institutions provided by the law and appoint or dismiss their directors, and settle other issues pertaining to state power.

Deputies' terms of office are four years. They must be at least twenty-five years old with a permanent residence in Lithuania. The last election was in 2016 and the next one will be in 2020.

THE PREAMBLE TO THE CONSTITUTION OF LITHUANIA

Not all national constitutions begin with a preamble, but many do. The preamble is an introduction that explains the purpose of the legal document, establishes its authority, describes the goals of the nation, and sets the tone for its government.

THE LITHUANIAN NATION
- *having created the State of Lithuania many centuries ago,*
- *having based its legal foundations on the Lithuanian Statutes and the Constitutions of the Republic of Lithuania,*
- *having for centuries staunchly defended its freedom and independence,*
- *having preserved its spirit, native language, writing, and customs,*
- *embodying the innate right of the human being and the Nation to live and create freely in the land of their fathers and forefathers—in the independent State of Lithuania,*
- *fostering national concord in the land of Lithuania,*
- *striving for an open, just, and harmonious civil society and State under the rule of law, by the will of the citizens of the reborn State of Lithuania, adopts and proclaims this ...*

The 2016 parliamentary election produced a surprise win for the Lithuanian Peasant and Greens Union (LVZS), which won fifty-four seats, the most seats of any one party. In the previous election, the party had won only one seat. The Peasant and Greens party is agrarian (pro-rural, pro-farmer) and environmentalist (green) in its political philosophy. The success of the party was attributed to voter dissatisfaction with established parties in light of persistent low wages, which had fueled rampant emigration, leading to a decline in Lithuania's population. The successful LVZS party formed a coalition government with the third-place party, the Social Democratic Party, after the second-place party, Homeland Union, declined to be part of the alliance.

The winning party chooses the prime minister and the speaker of the Seimas. In 2016, the new prime minister became Saulius Skvernelis. The new speaker of the Seimas, who presides over its meetings, became Viktoras Pranckietis. Both men are affiliated with the Peasant and Greens Union.

EXECUTIVE BRANCH

The executive branch includes the president as the chief of state and the prime minister as the head of government.

THE PRESIDENT The Lithuanian president is the highest official of the state. In 2009, Dalia Grybauskaite was elected president—the country's first woman president—and she was re-elected in 2014. She was also the first president to be elected to a second term. (The next election will be in 2019.) Grybauskaite was dubbed the "Lithuanian Iron Lady" by the international press in recognition of her steely resolve, outspoken style, and her black belt in karate. She speaks four languages in addition to her native tongue—English, Russian, Polish, and French.

Dalia Grybauskaite smiles during her presidential inauguration ceremony on July 12, 2009.

The president represents the country and is elected by citizens of Lithuania for a term of five years on the basis of universal suffrage by secret ballot (voting age is eighteen). The president upholds the constitution and the laws and also performs other duties:

- resolves major issues of foreign policy and conducts foreign policy jointly with the government
- signs international treaties, submitting them to the Seimas for ratification
- with the approval of the Seimas, appoints the prime minister and empowers him or her to form the government (Council of Ministers), and confirms its composition
- appoints and dismisses state officials
- submits candidates for the supreme court and the constitutional court for the evaluation of the Seimas

The Sąjūdis (Lithuanian Reform) movement won a majority in parliament in 1990, but a year later, as winter set in, many Lithuanians still had no heat or hot water in their homes. The voters were unhappy about unemployment, high prices, and fuel shortages, and when elections were held in October and November 1992, the pro-independence Lithuanian Democratic Labor Party (LDLP), formerly the Communist Party, was returned to power.

In 1993, the former head of the country's Communist Party, Algirdas Mykolas Brazauskas (1932–2010), was elected the first president of the newly independent Lithuania. He had been a major supporter of the Lithuanian independence movement, and had severed the country's Communist Party's links with Moscow. He served as president until 1998, and then decided to not run for re-election, and to retire from political life. He also resigned as a member of the LDLP.

In July 2001, however, Brazauskas made a comeback. He was appointed prime minister, a post he held until June 2006. Brazauskas served as chairman of the Lithuanian Social Democratic Party until May 2007, when he retired yet again. The following year he was diagnosed with cancer, and died in 2010, a much beloved figure in Lithuania. Lithuanian President Dalia Grybauskaitė said, "The memory of the first directly elected president of Lithuania … a strong and charismatic personality, will remain for a long time in the hearts of the Lithuanian people."

- with Seimas's approval, appoints and removes the chiefs of the armed forces and security service
- confers the highest military titles
- proclaims a state of emergency as provided by law
- makes annual reports to the Seimas on the "state of the nation" in Lithuania, including its domestic and foreign policy
- announces elections
- signs and announces laws passed by the Seimas, or sends them back to the Seimas for reconsideration
- issues acts and decrees
- exercises such other powers as provided by the constitution

THE PRIME MINISTER AND CABINET The executive government of Lithuania is composed of the prime minister and the cabinet, the fourteen-member Council of Ministers. The prime minister is appointed or dismissed by the president with the approval of the Seimas. Ministers are also appointed and dismissed by the president upon the recommendation of the prime minister.

The government controls affairs of the country, ensures state and civilian security, and carries out laws, resolutions of the Seimas on the enforcement of laws, and decrees of the president. It also enters into and maintains diplomatic relations with foreign countries and international organizations and performs the duties specified in the constitution and laws.

Since coming to power, the government has shouldered a twofold challenge. It has had to establish the legal, institutional, and regulatory framework of an independent democratic state. At the same time, it needed to restructure the centralized economy into a free-market economy while reducing economic dependence on the former Soviet Union.

THE JUDICIAL SYSTEM

The judicial system consists of a constitutional court, a supreme court, a court of appeals, and district and local courts. The constitutional court consists

of nine judges appointed for nonrenewable terms of nine years. It determines whether laws enacted by the Seimas, or actions of the president or Council of Ministers, are in conformity with the constitution.

The Seimas appoints three judges for the constitutional court and another three for the supreme court. Three judges for the court of appeals are appointed by the president with approval of the Seimas. Judges of district and local courts are appointed by the president. Public prosecutors conduct criminal cases on behalf of the state.

Lithuania's Constitutional Court issues a ruling in 2012.

INTERNET LINKS

https://www.constituteproject.org/constitution/Lithuania_2006.pdf?lang=en
This is a pdf of the 1992 Constitution of Lithuania, with amendments, in English.

https://www.lrp.lt/en
The official site of the president of Lithuania has biographical information about Dalia Grybauskaite as well as government news, available in English.

http://www.lrs.lt/sip/portal.show?p_k=2
This is the English language version of the official Seimas home site.

ECONOMY

Tall buildings define the business section of Vilnius.

4

LITHUANIA'S ECONOMY IS RELATIVELY small—it's only one-tenth the size of neighboring Poland's economy. But it has been growing quickly. Since 2000, it has doubled in size and is the largest economy of the Baltic states. The global economic crisis of 2008—2009 hit the country hard, but Lithuania has rebounded to become one of the fastest growing economies in Europe.

Lithuania joined the European Union (EU) in 2004—a political and economic union of twenty-eight European member states—and in 2015, became a part of the eurozone, meaning the country adopted the EU's common currency, the euro. This important move is intended to ensure greater economic stability and security, and to more firmly align itself with Europe and away from Russia. Whether this will have the desired results remains to be seen, however, as the EU itself faces challenges in the wake of Britain's 2016 vote to leave the union.

LIFE AFTER THE SOVIET UNION

The breakup of the Soviet Union in 1991 severely disrupted the economy of Lithuania. The Soviet Union had previously supplied Lithuania with heavily subsidized supplies of raw materials as well as guaranteed markets for the goods manufactured in Lithuania.

In 2011, some Lithuanian entrepreneurs worked with a French perfume company to create Lietuvos Kvapas, ("the scent of Lithuania") in an effort to improve the country's image abroad. The fragrance, a combination of wildflowers, ginger, raspberry, sandalwood, tree moss, and musk, is not meant to be worn but is more of an air freshener. The product is mainly aimed at tourists.

A banner hung on the headquarters of the European Commission in Brussels welcomes Lithuania into the Eurozone on January 5, 2015.

After gaining its independence from the Soviet Union in September 1991, Lithuania made steady progress in developing a market economy. It received considerable international support for its economic reform by gaining membership into the International Monetary Fund (IMF) and World Bank in 1992. The European Bank for Reconstruction and Development, the World Bank, and the IMF guaranteed loans to bolster the recovering nation's economy.

To ensure economic stability after the breakup of the Soviet Union, Lithuania and the other two Baltic states, Latvia and Estonia, launched a program of land reform and market-oriented economic reforms. The economic changes affected price structure, government spending, foreign trade, banking and monetary policy, competition, taxes, ownership, and privatization laws. The great majority of state property was been privatized, and trade became more diversified, with a gradual drifting away from the former Soviet Union to international markets, mostly within the European Union (EU).

During the Soviet occupation, 5 percent of its exports were sent to the West; in 2005 exports to the EU were nearer to 65 percent. A main reason for the shift in export focus to the West was the collapse of the Russian ruble in 1998. Lithuania's economy fell into negative growth, and budget deficits amassed. As the economy recovered from the crisis, Lithuania looked West for its trading partners.

In 2015, Lithuania's gross domestic product (GDP) stood at $41.27 billion. GDP is an economic statistic that measures the value of a country's total production of goods and services in a given year. Economists use the figure to evaluate the condition of a nation's economy.

Like other post-industrialized nations, Lithuania's economic profile shows a strong inclination toward the services sector, which includes transportation, shipping, and the wholesale and retail trade. Principal exports and imports

KALININGRAD, A LITTLE BIT OF RUSSIA

Nestled on the Baltic Coast between Lithuania and Poland, the Kaliningrad Oblast maintains an unusual distinction. This 5,800-sq-mile (15,100 sq km) chunk of territory is not a country unto itself. Rather, it's an exclave, or isolated section, of Russia, with which it shares no boundaries. An oblast is a term dating from the time of the Soviet Union, describing an administrative district or zone.

In this oblast, the main city is Kaliningrad, which prior to 1946 was called Konigsberg, a city in the state of Prussia. A region with a long, complex history, which was part of the German Empire before World War II, Prussia no longer exists. After the dissolution of Prussia after the war, the city was renamed Kaliningrad and the district became an oblast of the Soviet Union.

Today, the Kaliningrad Oblast is Russia's only ice-free port on the Baltic Sea, which makes it logistically very important. Its population is almost entirely Russian, and for those people to travel to Russia proper, they must traverse Lithuania. In 2003, Lithuania and Russia  *officially defined their 141-mile (227 km) boundary, in accordance with a land and maritime treaty. A stone monument marks the three-point juncture of Lithuania, Poland, and Russia. Today, Lithuania operates a simplified transit system for Russian nationals traveling to and from the Kaliningrad region.*

are mineral products, machinery and equipment, chemicals, and light industrial products such as textiles and food products. The country's current main trade partners are Russia, Germany, Poland, Latvia, Estonia, the Netherlands, Sweden, the United States, the United Kingdom, France, and Denmark.

Lithuania has a skilled workforce with expertise in modern technology developed during the years when the Baltic states were exploited as an economic and industrial laboratory by the Soviet Union. Its total workforce stood at nearly 1.5 million in 2015, with a majority employed in the services sector (66.6 percent).

Tethered cows stand in a grassy field in the Kupiskis district of northeastern Lithuania.

AGRICULTURE AND FISHING

Lithuania has always been agriculturally self-sufficient. In recent times, though, there has been a drop in agricultural production as Lithuania focused its attention more toward a service-based economy. Agriculture contributes a mere 3.2 percent of the country's GDP today, but provides employment for almost 8 percent of the workforce. Of a total land area of 16 million acres (6.5 million ha), only 4.32 million acres (1.75 million ha) are used for food and feed crops.

The most important sector of the farming industry is livestock. Cattle, sheep, pigs, and chickens provide meat, eggs, and dairy products for export as well as domestic consumption.

Wheat, barley, and oats are grown in the western and central part of the country. Potatoes and sugar beets are also valuable products. Flax is an important product of the eastern part of the country. The stalks of this plant are used to make linen cloth, and flaxseeds are used as a dietary supplement and to produce linseed oil.

The fishing industry is also profitable. Herring, cod, and flounder are caught in the Baltic Sea, the Barents Sea, and the Atlantic Ocean. Carp and eel come from Lithuania's many bountiful inland lakes and ponds.

Lithuania was once known as the Amber Coast because of its great deposits of amber, a translucent fossilized tree resin valued for its subtle beauty. Amber can be found scattered like pebbles along the beaches of the Baltic shores. For centuries it was a source of wealth for the Balts, who traded it as far away as Egypt. Tutankhamen's

tomb included jewelry made with amber. A peculiarity of the resin is that before hardening, the ooze attracts insects, which may become trapped inside. In some specimens of amber, perfectly preserved insects from ages past can be found fossilized inside.

INDUSTRIES

The main branches of Lithuania's industry are oil processing, machinery and transportation equipment manufacturing, electronics, textiles, chemicals, plastics, forest products, and food processing. Food processing is primarily based on local meat and dairy supplies. Other industries include the production and packing of sugar, bread, confectionery, alcoholic products, tobacco, and vegetable oil.

Vilnius and Kaunas are industrial centers, with textile mills producing knitwear, carpets, stockings, leather goods, footwear, and linen, cotton, and silk fabrics. Substantial amounts of these products are exported to other European countries. Šiauliai, the fourth-largest Lithuanian city, is an industrial center for the production of foodstuffs and beverages, precision lathes, television parts and components, computers, and bicycles.

Lithuania produces television and audio equipment, refrigerators, vacuum cleaners, electric engines, drills, and some agricultural machinery. The construction materials industry is based on local raw materials and satisfies local needs in cement, brick, glass, roofing supplies, thermal insulation, and nonmetal substances. Cement and bricks are also exported. The chemical industry, dependent entirely on imported raw materials, specializes in fertilizers, plastics, household chemicals, and rubber products. Local timber is processed for both local consumption and export markets.

TRANSPORTATION

Transportation in Lithuania is good and continually improving. The Via Baltica, the highway that links Lithuania to Latvia and Estonia in the north and to Poland in the south, runs through Lithuania via Kaunas. Major airline flights arrive daily at Vilnius International Airport, the largest of four commercial airports in the country.

In the same period, the railways carried some 6.98 million people and 45.6 million tons of freight. Railway lines crisscross the country, totaling 1,242 miles (1,998 km). The Jonava railway station, a short distance from Kaunas's Karmelava International Airport, links to the Kaliningrad Region, Latvia, and the Klaipeda Seaport for convenient passenger and cargo transportation.

Vilnius is a transportation hub, with modern rail networks.

The port of Klaipeda is ice-free and operates year-round. It's the most important Lithuanian transportation hub, connecting sea, land, and railway routes from East to West.

With these integrated transport systems, a key geographical position, and the historical relationship with the former Soviet republics, Lithuania is of considerable interest to Western companies. IBM, DHL, Xerox, Olivetti, and Minolta have come to Lithuania. Other key foreign investors include Scandinavian TeliaSonera (telecommunications), Paroc (construction materials), Storaenso (wood products), DSV (sea transport), American Kraft Foods and Mars (food processing), and Philip Morris (tobacco products). German car giant Volkswagen-Audi and French carmakers Renault and Peugeot have opened showrooms, the Swiss Vast Group has opened a chain of stores across the country, and Scandinavian companies are initiating joint ventures.

INTERNET LINKS

http://www.baltic21.org/economy/lithuania.html
Devoted to the countries of the Baltic region, this site gives an overview of Lithuania's economy.

https://www.cia.gov/library/publications/the-world-factbook/geos/lh.html
The CIA World Factbook provides up-to-date information about Lithuania's economy.

http://www.heritage.org/index/country/lithuania
The Index of Economic Freedom evaluates Lithuania's economic reforms.

http://www.truelithuania.com/topics/history-and-politics-of-lithuania/economy-of-lithuania
This site gives an overview of Lithuania's economy and tax structure.

ENVIRONMENT

Bicyclists relax by the Baltic Sea in Nida, a resort town on the Curonian Spit.

5

S INCE ACHIEVING INDEPENDENCE, Lithuania has been conscientiously tackling its pressing environmental issues. This has been a huge challenge, since the Lithuanian landscape, like those of most countries of the former Soviet Union, suffered from many years of neglect and abuse. Political apathy and general technological backwardness throughout the Soviet years resulted in damaging environmental problems that continue to the present day.

In 2012, Yale University declared Lithuania to be the country with the best forest protection and management system in the world, over the previous fifteen year period.

Some of the measures undertaken included establishing a realistic system of waste management, the cleanup of contaminated military sites, and the establishment of parks and nature reserves. Lithuania is working hard to ensure the continued preservation and sustainability of its environment. Some of the country's environmental management bodies include the Ministry of Environmental Protection, established in 1994; the Department of Land Management and Biological Diversity; and the Joint Research Center. Another organization that helps in the support and realization of environmental projects is the Lithuanian Environmental Investment Fund. All environmental entities in Lithuania comply with the Environmental Strategy of the Republic of Lithuania, taking into account the norms and standards of the European Union.

SOVIET LEGACY

Aggressive industrial production through the use of chemical fertilizer and pesticides during the Soviet years seriously contaminated Lithuania's soil with biogenic and toxic chemicals. Scant attention was paid to soil pollution in the pursuit of agricultural gains.

Former Soviet military activities and their use of oil products and heavy metals left 167,444 acres (67,762 ha) of Lithuanian land contaminated. The cleanup of these military sites, leading to the reutilization of the land, is a costly, ongoing project, even with funds from the EU.

NUCLEAR ENERGY

In the recent past, Lithuania was heavily dependent on the Ignalina nuclear power plant to supply its industries with the necessary power. The plant, built during the Soviet era, was run on two powerful reactors, providing 87 percent of Lithuania's total energy needs. The plant became outdated, however, and was similar in construction to the Chernobyl plant in Ukraine that exploded in 1986, with catastrophic results. The EU, therefore, insisted that Lithuania shut down the plant as one of the conditions to the country's entry into the union. The first reactor, Ignalina I, was shut down in 2005, and the second, Ignalina 2, in 2009. The governments of Estonia, Latvia, Lithuania, and Poland agreed in 2006 to construct a new nuclear power plant together at Ignalina, but as of 2016, the project has not yet broken ground.

ENERGY ALTERNATIVES

Without the nuclear power plant, Lithuania needed to find other sources of energy, as the country is severely lacking in fuel resources. For example, Lithuania doesn't have natural gas resources of its own, and all its gas is

The outdated Ignalina nuclear power plant is no longer functioning.

imported from Russia by way of a single pipeline from Belarus. Lithuania has also become highly dependent on imported electricity, and therefore, consumers find their electric bills to be quite high. But that situation may be changing. In 2015, new transmission lines connected Lithuania to Sweden and Poland. Once in operation, the effect of the Lithuanian-Sweden power link was immediately reflected in lower electricity prices.

Lithuania has yet to reach its potential in developing such renewable energy sources as hydropower (water), solar, wind, and geothermal power, but it is working toward that goal. In 2010, about 19.7 percent of its overall energy came from renewable sources. The country expects renewables to generate 23 percent of its total power by 2020. The Kaunas Hydroelectric Power Plant, located on the Nemunas River, supplies about 3 percent of Lithuania's electrical needs. That station, along with the Lithuanian Power Plant, the Kaunas Combined Heat and Power plant, and Lithuania's electrical transmission grid are all undergoing modernization to increase their power-generating and -delivery capacity.

A solar farm in Lithuania produces green energy.

WATER AND SANITATION

Lithuania is one of the few countries in Europe using groundwater resources as its only source of potable water. Yet nearly a perturbing third of the country's water, including rivers and lakes, is polluted. Uncontrolled dumping by industries and the lack of sewage treatment facilities are the main causes of water pollution. Experts estimate that Lithuania's largest inland body of water, the Curonian Lagoon, is about 85 percent contaminated with effluents from industrial and domestic waste.

This is because of the high population density around the Baltic coast, and the industrial center of Klaipeda is just north of the lagoon. As the Curonian Lagoon lies just inside the eastern shoreline of the Baltic Sea, runoff currents from the sea are common, bringing in with them additional pollution from neighboring Russia and Poland. Industrial waste from Belarus also pollutes rivers that flow into the Curonian Lagoon. However, since the 1990s, the flow of pollutants into the lagoon has been significantly reduced.

The completion of the wastewater treatment plant in Klaipeda has also helped to reduce the concentration of pollutants in the lagoon. In all, five sources of pollution have been eliminated, and pollution was prevented in

A small fishing boat is moored in the Curonian Lagoon.

a 148-acre (60-ha) area. Between 1998 and 2005, Lithuania also managed to halve the concentration of pollutants in the Baltic Sea near its coast.

Wastewater quality after treatment is rapidly improving. In 2012, up to 97 percent of wastewater from households and industry had been cleaned to the appropriate standards.

WASTE

Until quite recently, most of Lithuania's municipal waste was disposed of in landfills. However, many of those municipal landfills were neither environmentally friendly nor properly operated. Flammable hazardous wastes, including solvents and materials polluted with oil, were incinerated in boilers ill equipped to do the job. Beginning in 2009, old, noncompliant landfills began to shut down and by 2012, all of the country's eight hundred such landfills were closed.

A proper system of waste management has only recently been established. New domestic dump sites are being set up in Kedainiai and Kaisiadorys, and major Lithuanian cities have begun to use separate containers for glass, plastics, metals, and kitchen waste. With financial backing from the EU, Lithuania will be able to install modern waste management infrastructure in most of its major cities. In 2013, the National Strategic Waste Management Plan was put into place ensure the country's rapid adoption of improved facilities and systems to further clean and protect the environment.

AIR POLLUTION

One of the relatively new environmental concerns that Lithuania faces today is air pollution from cars and trucks. Although the quality of air in recent times has improved somewhat, at one point about a third of Lithuanian

A heap of trash in a city park awaits cleanup by environmentally-minded volunteers.

PROTECTED AREAS

About 15 percent of Lithuania's land lies in protected areas. There are three nature reserves (Cepkeliai, Kamanos, Viesvile), two cultural reserves (Kernave and Vilnius Castles), five national parks (Aukštaitija, Dzūkija, the Curonian Spit, Žemaitija, and Trakai Historic National Park), thirty regional parks, the Zuvintas Biosphere Reserve, and other protected areas.

Three sites are included on the UNESCO World Heritage list—the Curonian Spit, the Old Town of Vilnius, and the Archaeological Site of Kernavė.

The nature reserves are home to many species of animals and plants. A special permit is required to even enter these reserves.

A wooden path into the Grey Dunes makes for easy hiking on the Curonian Spit.

The Čepkeliai Reserve, in southern Lithuania, established in 1975, has the country's largest and oldest marshland. A wide variety of berries, birds, insects, and reptiles find haven at this reserve.

The Kamanos Reserve in northern Lithuania was established in 1979. Under protection are its bogs, 556 species of higher plants, and 123 species of mosses. Twenty-six of those plants are noted as rare or endangered species. Wildlife is also diverse, with 36 species of mammals, 120 species of birds, 3 species of reptiles, 6 species of amphibians, and two species of fish. Access to this park is carefully monitored, and any type of commercial activity is strictly prohibited.

Established in 1991, the Viesvile Reserve in the Karsuva lowland includes 7,947 acres (3,216 ha) of great natural beauty. The reserve has a uniquely homogeneous ecosystem as it was hardly touched by Lithuania's economic activity in the Soviet interval.

The fourth protected area, the Zuvintas Biosphere Reserve, is composed of 30,678 acres (12,415 ha) of woodlands, marshes, and water. It was established in 1937 to preserve the flora and fauna of Zuvintas Lake as well as its bogs and swamps. Some 250 species of birds such as the heron and mute swan can be found there.

territory was suffused with polluted air at any given time. Tons of pollutants from vehicles are released into the atmosphere each year. In Vilnius, traffic congestion has become acute, especially during the morning and evening rush hours.

The other main sources of air pollution are industrial centers and cities such as Vilnius, Kaunas, Klaipeda, and Jonava, where fertilizer and cement factories as well as power plants are concentrated. The Šiauliai region is the most heavily polluted in Lithuania, contributing 40 percent of the general emissions for the entire country because of the presence of a thermal power plant.

An electric car charges at a power supply station in Vilnius.

Air pollution not only damaged more than two-thirds of the nation's forests but also added to the problem of acid rain. Forests affected by acid rain are found in the vicinity of Jonava, Mažeikiai, and Elektrėnai, Lithuania's main chemical and energy generating sites.

In June 2005 the government approved a strategy for the development of the Lithuanian transportation system. Some of the aims include tightening the requirements for exhaust gases and noise levels; prohibiting car traffic in old towns, central parts of cities, and centers of high-density parking; encouraging the use of clean fuel; and promoting the use of electric vehicles and hybrid vehicles for city travel. The government has also set up the Sustainable Development Strategy for its industrial sector.

The amount of main air emissions in 2011 fell by 7 percent compared to the previous year. This indicates a successful implementation of cleaner technologies in industry. Annual greenhouse gas emissions are among the lowest in the EU. Lithuania has signed treaties to reduce its greenhouse gas emissions and to gradually reduce and prevent air pollution. It also has ratified treaties on climate change and ozone layer protection.

The Neris River winds through forestland.

LITHUANIA'S FORESTS

Forests are of great economic, ecological, cultural, and social importance to the people of Lithuania. Forests cover about 33 percent, or about 4.9 million acres (2 million ha), of the entire country. The state manages about 50 percent of these forests, and some 30 percent are held in private hands. The rest of the state forestland is reserved for possible future privatization.

Lithuania's Law on Forests was approved in 2001. The law calls for forest management that includes equal regeneration, protection, and use regardless of ownership. One of the conditions of the law states that clear-cut forest areas must be reforested within three years after cutting.

Many of Lithuania's original animal and plant species are now extinct because of past indifference. Acid rain due to air pollution from industries and power plants from neighboring countries is also a contributing factor. Nevertheless, Lithuania is determined to preserve its forests' riches. Some of Lithuania's recent triumphs include a substantial increase of woodlands, an enlargement of protected areas, and the preservation of biological diversity. Lithuania also adheres to the Ramsar Convention, protecting wetlands, biodiversity, and the conservation of endangered species.

INTERNET LINKS

http://www.baltic21.org/environment/lithuania.html
This site provides a quick overview of Lithuania's main environmental issues.

http://www.eea.europa.eu/soer-2015/countries/lithuania
The European Environment Agency site evaluates Lithuania's progress in environmental matters.

http://epi.yale.edu/country/lithuania
The Environmental Performance Index evaluates and ranks Lithuania's progress in nine environmental indicators.

http://www.gmu.lt/lithuanian_state_forests
The Directorate General of State Forests provides general information on Lithuania's forests.

http://www.world-nuclear.org/information-library/country-profiles/countries-g-n/lithuania.aspx
This site gives an in-depth, up-to-date look at nuclear power in Lithuania.

LITHUANIANS

Two girls in traditional dress take part in the Europeade Festival of European folk culture in Klaipeda, Lithuania.

ETHNICALLY, LITHUANIANS ARE A fairly homogenous people—in fact, they are the least diverse population in the Baltic countries. Ethnic Lithuanians make up the large majority of people, some 84 percent in 2011. Remarkably, today's Lithuanians are genetically quite similar to the people who lived in the region during the Neolithic period more than four thousand years ago. They are also closely related to the Indo-European settlers who arrived in the Baltic region around 2500 BCE.

Those ancient people organized into several tribes, and in the course of time these tribes merged, generating today's ethnic Lithuanians. The tribes were the Lithuanians, the Jotvings in the Suvalkija region, the Semigallians and the Selonians in the north, the Curonians in the far west, and the Samogitians (or Zemaitians), who inhabited the Žemaitija region. Today these tribes and their descendants—the people of Lithuania and Latvia—are referred to as Balts. This term was derived from the name of the Baltic Sea and was first applied during the nineteenth century.

From the thirteenth century, Lithuania was settled by other nationalities as well, including Poles, Germans, Russians, and Tatars

People gather in a Vilnius city square on a clear April day.

(Mongols). At the beginning of the fourteenth century many Jews settled in Lithuania, where they found asylum from religious persecution in other European countries. In the second half of the eighteenth century, Russian Orthodox Christians also seeking sanctuary from such persecution settled in Lithuanian villages.

The character of today's Lithuanians has been influenced by decades of intense Soviet repression. Many talented and educated Lithuanians fled the country in 1944, and many more died under harsh German and Soviet occupations. In spite of a concerted attempt to stamp out Lithuanian culture and identity, the Lithuanians have cherished their traditions and still point proudly to the historical greatness of their country. They feel themselves to be the natural leaders of the Baltic region, although they may also feel some apprehension about what the future holds for their struggling new country.

The population of Lithuania is about 2,854,000 (in 2016), and has been declining. Ten years earlier, it stood at an estimated 3.6 million. Ethnic Lithuanians make up the majority (84.1 percent), distantly followed by the

Poles (6.6 percent). Most of the Poles reside in Vilnius and southeastern Lithuania. Russians, who live mainly in urban areas such as Visaginas, Vilnius, and Klaipeda, form the third-largest ethnic group (5.8 percent). People of other ethnic groups are few: Belorusians (1.2 percent) and others, such as Latvians, Jews, Tatars, Gypsies, and Germans together (4.4 percent), make up the rest.

POLES

The Polish presence in Lithuania dates back to the Middle Ages, when Grand Duke Jogaila's marriage to the Polish princess Jadwiga joined the two countries. Many upper-class Lithuanians adopted the Polish language and Polish customs, and the distinction between the two groups became blurred. Until World War II, ethnic Lithuanians were a small minority in Vilnius, fewer than the Poles and the Jews. Many important Polish cultural figures came from Vilnius, such as writers Czeslaw Milosz and Adam Mickiewicz, and Jozef Pilsudski, the ruler of Poland between the world wars.

As a result of the historical conflict between the two countries over Vilnius, many Lithuanians used to fear that the Poles wanted to reclaim Vilnius. In turn, their anxiety about Lithuanian nationalism impelled many Poles to support the Soviets during the independence struggle, another factor that further aggravated relations. International treaties signed in the 1990s have ended this prolonged conflict and eased relations.

RUSSIANS

Lithuanian Russians mostly migrated to Lithuania after World War II, a time when Lithuania underwent rapid industrialization. The 2011 national census counted 176,913 Russians living in the country. About 50 percent of the population in the Visaginas municipality is ethnic Russian. Most of them belong to the Russian Orthodox Church. Because of the painful Soviet occupation, some resentment toward Russians lingers among ethnic Lithuanians. The problem is not as acute as it is in the other Baltic states, however, where the percentage of Russians is much higher.

The Memorial of the Victims of Nazism at the Ninth Fort in Kaunas, Lithuania, built in 1984, features dramatic sculptural forms. During the German occupation, the Nazis used Kaunas Fortress for the mass execution of Jews and other prisoners.

THE JERUSALEM OF THE NORTH

Jews began settling in Lithuania in the fourteenth century, when they were invited in by Grand Duke Vytautus. By the eighteenth century, Lithuania was considered to be one of the most important centers of Jewish culture in the world. Vilnius was known as the "Jerusalem of the North" because of its large Jewish presence—30 percent of the population of the worldly capital—with a large number of synagogues and Hebrew schools. At the time, Jews made up 7.6 percent of the Lithuanian population. Later in the eighteenth century, Vilnius was a center of Jewish Orthodox resistance to the Hasidic movement then sweeping Eastern Europe, and before World War II, Vilnius was the hub of Yiddish publishing.

The Jewish community was almost entirely obliterated by the Nazis during the German occupation of Lithuania. About 95 percent of Lithuanian Jews were killed, a higher percentage than in any other Jewish community in Europe More than 130,000 Vilnius Jews died, and the rich Jewish culture that had flourished in Vilnius since the Middle Ages was wiped out. The Nazis interned and exterminated Jews at Fort Nine, a Nazi concentration camp in Lithuania, only a few miles outside Kaunas. In addition, Jews from all over Europe were herded there to await execution. The prison cells still exist, and there is now a museum and a monument to the victims on the site.

In 1989 there were just some 12,400 Jews in the entire country. Many of those Jews who were not killed in the Holocaust had joined the steady flow of emigrants away from the Baltic states. Apart from economic reasons, the urge to emigrate was also provoked by memories of Lithuanian participation

TATARS

Some fifty thousand to one hundred thousand Tatars, also known as Mongols, came to Lithuania during the time of Vytautas the Great (1350–1430), who was their protector. The Tatars were renowned for their valor in battle—their main occupation became fighting the enemies of Lithuania. In return, Lithuanian rulers gave them protection and religious freedom. Later, the Tatars took up agriculture, animal husbandry, and the processing of animal skins. A famous Lithuanian Tatar was General Maciej Sulkiewicz, who headed the Cabinet of Ministers of the Republic of Crimea in 1918. In 1997, the six hundredth anniversary of the settlement of Tatars in the Grand Duchy of Lithuania was celebrated. A year later, a spiritual center was reestablished for the ethnic Tatars' Sunni Muslims.

in the Holocaust—the first massacres in Lithuania were conducted entirely by Lithuanians without direct German involvement—and by perceptions of contemporary anti-Semitism. Today only about four thousand Jews live in Lithuania. Their communities are concentrated mainly in Vilnius, with smaller ones in Kaunas, Klaipeda, and Šiauliai. A Jewish studies program has recently been established at Vilnius University.

TRADITIONAL DRESS

The Lithuanian national costume dates only from the early nineteenth century, although it differs considerably from one region to another in ornamentation and color. From the early twentieth century, the national dress, particularly for women, has been influenced by urban tastes. Today it is usually worn by participants in folk music and dance concerts and in religious processions and ethnic festivals and processions.

A folk festival in Klaipeda provides an occasion to wear traditional clothing.

Most garments are produced commercially according to designs drawn by professionals, but the tradition of making one's own is again becoming popular.

Men's traditional clothing consists of a shirt, trousers, vest, lightweight coat or jacket, overcoat or sheepskin coat, hat, and footwear. Shirts are full-sleeved and made of thick linen, with a cotton stand-up collar embroidered in black and red. Before the twentieth century, trousers were made of homespun linen, wool, or cotton. Winter trousers are dark-colored, and summer ones are white or white on blue. They are tied with a sash around the waist. Strips of cord or leather are appliquéd to the edging, cuffs, collars, and pockets of coats and jackets, which are worn over vests. Many kinds of caps are worn by men in rural areas, but in warm weather straw hats are preferred.

There are several kinds of traditional footwear in the countryside, but the most striking shoes are perhaps the solid wooden *klumpes* (KLOOM-pus), worn by men and women.

In the past, the clothing of a Lithuanian woman reflected her industry, accomplishment, and taste. Traditional woman's dress consists of a skirt, blouse, bodice (a tight sleeveless garment worn over the blouse), apron, and sash. Outer garments are a sheepskin coat and a scarf. Unmarried women generally wear ribbons and beads in their hair instead of scarves.

Women of the Aukštaitija region prefer light colors, particularly white. Their skirts are mostly checked, and the aprons have horizontal red patterns at the bottom. The background of an apron is usually checked, striped, or patterned in cat-paw motifs. The fronts of blouses, sleeves, collars, and cuffs are embellished with red stripes.

The Zemaitian women's attire includes several articles of sharply contrasting colors—a tailored bodice, a vertically striped skirt, and an apron. Shawls are worn over the head and shoulders. *Klumpes* are the typical Zemaitian footwear.

Women's traditional clothes in the Klaipeda region are dark in color, and the blouses have a gathered neckline. The bottom portion of sleeves, the cuffs, and a wide band below the shoulders have colorful designs such as clovers, tulips, or oak leaves. Their sashes and stoles have intricate patterns. The stole is made of two panels with a narrow lengthwise insertion embroidered with white plant motifs. Almost all women carry a decorative handbag called a *delmonas* (dayl-MOH-nus), which is fastened at the front or side of the waistband.

INTERNET LINKS

https://www.cia.gov/library/publications/the-world-factbook/geos/lh.html
This US government site has up to date information about the people and society of Lithuania.

http://goeasteurope.about.com/od/lithuaniatravel/ss/Lithuanian-Folk-Costumes.htm
This captioned photo gallery shows colorful Lithuanian folk costumes.

http://www.truelithuania.com/topics/culture-of-lithuania/ethnicities-of-lithuania
A good overview of the majority and minority ethnic groups in Lithuania is presented on this page.

LIFESTYLE

A traditional Lithuanian wooden house is a typical home in the village of Pervalka.

7

L IVING THROUGH THE RAPID transition from soviet-style life to that of a newly independent nation has been like cultural whiplash to many Lithuanians. Almost overnight, the entire country switched its gaze from east to west. The nation exchanged its identity from Russian with a Soviet mindset to European with a more Western sensibility. Joining the European Union in 2004 only added to Lithuania's new perception of itself as a European nation.

The rapid changes—from domination to independence, from communist to democratic—have been tough on many people, especially older folks. The transformation affects many parts of life, the economic, political, cultural, social, and even the personal. Younger people have been more flexible, optimistic, and enthusiastic about embracing a Western lifestyle. At the same time, many Lithuanians want to get in touch with their heritage and unique national identity, which in some cases means returning to old ways and figuring out how to incorporate them into modern life.

The cost of living in Lithuania, not including rent, is 38 percent lower than in the United States (as of 2016). Rents in Lithuania, on average, are 68 percent lower.

A farmer harvests wheat in rural Telšiai.

RURAL LIVING

Rural living has always been an important part of the Lithuanian way of life. Today, many of the old Soviet collectives have been broken up into small farms, but the process has not been an easy one. Rural people who had only ever experienced the ideas of communal property and collective work under the Soviet system had trouble understanding new ways of doing things. The concepts of private property, individual initiative, and personal responsibility were hard for them to grasp. Simply returning to small family farm ownership proved to be difficult because the people basically didn't know how to do it.

In addition, the demands of membership in the EU required Lithuanian farmers to modernize. Large-scale farming by educated agricultural professionals is what is now required, and the common rural folk have largely been unable to keep up. The result has been that fewer rural people earn their livings in the agricultural sector.

URBAN LIFE

This aerial view shows an urban housing project in Vilnius.

Most Lithuanians live in cities and towns. Around 66.5 percent dwell in the five largest cities—Vilnius, Kaunas, Klaipeda, Šiauliai, and Panevėžys.

After World War II the urban population grew steadily as the cities were rebuilt and new industries sprang up. Today, housing is a mix of single-family houses and apartment buildings.

The Soviet regime built the huge housing projects that now surround almost every town in the Baltic region. These mass-produced and badly assembled concrete towers are very different from the attractive, historic city centers that tourists visit. Faced with a chronic lack of housing, families still live in cramped accommodations, sometimes with members of their extended family or even sharing a kitchen and bathroom with other families in communal apartments. More and more families are leaving the urban centers for newer, single-family homes in the suburbs. In 2014, the urban population numbers were declining by 1 percent annually.

Street crime is a problem in the cities, and car thefts and break-ins are not uncommon. Still, conditions are better than those in many parts of the former Soviet Union. Public transportation in the cities is well developed, with buses being the most common means of getting around. Lithuania has the most advanced telephone system in the former Soviet Union, and unlike some cities in neighboring countries, it is safe to drink the tap water.

THE ROLE OF WOMEN

Lithuania was the first country in Europe to define the rights of women not simply as mothers or potential mothers. This was the result of a matrilineal tradition in the ancient tribes and a society in which men were absent during long periods of war. The Statute of Lithuania of 1529 established the principle of individual legal responsibility and equality for women in the eyes of the law, irrespective of religion or marital status.

In present-day Lithuania, women work in all occupations. Wage discrimination on the grounds of sex, age, race, nationality, or political convictions is illegal. Still, women's participation in political life and public administration is not on par with men's. The number of women in parliament since independence has never been more than 20 percent. In the 2016 election, 31.2 percent of the candidates running for office were women; thirty women were elected to the 141-seat parliament.

THE FAMILY

Prior to World War II, many extended families, composed of grandparents, parents, children, uncles, aunts, and their children, lived and worked together as units in villages. Often servants and other nonrelatives lived in the house and were treated as part of the family. Extended families are still found, both in cities and the countryside, as a result of the prolonged housing shortage.

Today, however, most Lithuanian families are nuclear families, consisting of a married couple and their children. The father is usually the head of the household. Given the rise of single-parent families today, though, many single mothers are now the head of the household.

Traditionally, a woman went to live with her husband's family when she married, and daughters-in-law were readily welcomed as members of the family.

BIRTH

It is still thought that evil spirits and improper behavior can harm an unborn baby or the expectant mother. For these reasons, pregnant women have to observe a number of restrictions. At the same time, family, friends, and neighbors—in fact the whole village—protect and indulge the whims and fancies of expectant mothers.

Childbirth is shrouded in secrecy, and people talk of pregnancy and the actual birth by using such euphemisms as "The oven fell apart at Petra's" or "It is a joyous day at Antana's."

The birth of a child is considered a blessing. Soon after the birth, the women among the new parents' relatives and neighbors visit the mother and child. Each visitor brings a symbolic gift. No visitor comes empty-handed, as that is considered to jeopardize the child's good fortune. In many areas, it is customary to bring an omelet or a buckwheat loaf.

A child's christening is held two or more weeks after the birth. Godmothers and godfathers play important roles in the event. The selection of these godparents is considered crucial because it is thought that the child absorbs their temperaments and habits. This process binds families together, as the godparents take on part of the responsibility of raising the child.

CHILDHOOD RITUALS

It is through ritual introduction to adult responsibilities that the young are considered to have come of age.

The baking of her first loaf of bread marks the onset of puberty and is the symbol of a girl's coming of age. On a Friday evening, the mother gives some rye flour to her daughter. The daughter mixes the dough and leaves it to ferment overnight. On Saturday morning, the girl kneads the dough, then allows it to rise. She lights the oven, forms the loaves, incises a cross on the top of the first, and puts the loaves in the oven. When they are done, she removes them. The bread is eaten that day by her family with great ceremony.

In rural areas, fathers teach their sons how to harness and unharness horses, yoke and unyoke oxen, and to plow their first furrow alone.

GOING TO SCHOOL

A new national education system was introduced in Lithuania in 1990. Education is compulsory from ages six until sixteen, and is free of charge at all levels. General schools go from six to fourteen years, and secondary schools from fifteen to seventeen years. Lithuanian is the main language of instruction, although there are schools at which classes are taught in English, Russian, Polish, or Yiddish, with some schools offering classes in two or more languages. There are twenty-seven institutions of higher education in Lithuania, including the venerable Vilnius University, Vytautas Magnus

Students study in the light-filled library at Vilnius University.

EXECUTING THE MATCHMAKER

Arranging marriages with the help of the matchmaker was once widely practiced in Lithuania, but today the young choose their own life partners and matchmakers rarely play a part in their social lives and courtship. Nowadays, matchmakers are only characters acted out at weddings to bring fun to the occasion.

A wedding tradition that has survived is the mock execution of the matchmaker. The bride's friends and siblings decide that the matchmaker had exaggerated the description of the groom's looks and possessions, so they decide to execute the matchmaker. The sentence varies—he may be condemned to be burned by water, or frozen to death on the stove, or to be sent away to a hayloft with all the girls of the neighborhood. He accepts his sentence and asks to be allowed to say good-bye to all the ladies. He then smears his face with soot and tries to kiss every woman and girl in the house. The wittier the matchmaker, the funnier is his "execution." In the end, the bride's mother takes pity on the poor man, and as a sign of her forgiveness throws a towel across his shoulders. The matchmaker is thus saved, and the guests hang a dummy instead.

University in Kaunas, Vilnius Technical University, and the Lithuanian Academy of Sciences. Vilnius University, founded in 1579, was the first university in Eastern Europe. Today it is the largest university in Lithuania.

Adult literacy is very high—99.8 percent for both men and women. In 2012, 4.8 percent of the GDP was spent on education, about the same percentage as its neighboring Baltic countries.

WEDDINGS

Modern Lithuanian weddings are full of humor and good-natured teasing. Although they have been simplified, they retain the main elements of traditional weddings.

After a civil ceremony and a solemn wedding in the church, the wedding party heads for the bride's home for a feast. The way is barred, however, by the bride's family and friends with ropes of flowers. The last of the garlands is stretched across her parents' gate. The groom's friends buy their passage with candy and a bottle of whiskey. They also distribute candy to children along the way.

The bride's parents meet the newlyweds at their threshold with bread, salt, and wine glasses filled with water—all symbolic of a fulfilled life.

Inside, the seats for the bride and groom are adorned with more flowers and garlands, but they cannot sit down as the chairs are already occupied by neighbors dressed as gypsies, a matchmaker, a bride (a man in disguise), or a bridegroom (a woman in disguise). Both groups start haggling over the price of the seats, and after much banter and laughter the seats are sold for a bottle of whiskey.

One dish is deliberately made bitter, and on the first bite the guests start singing a traditional song: "Bitter, bitter is the food. It will be sweet when the bridegroom kisses the bride." The guests then volunteer lots of instructions to the bridegroom on how to do it well.

A very important wedding role is played by the matron of honor, who is usually a married woman closely related to the bride. She remains next to

A bride and groom walk through the city in Klaipėda.

the bride and groom, making sure all the customs are followed, and acts as a symbolic guardian to the bridal pair to ensure that no evil might damage their health and fertility.

At the end of the reception, the bride says good-bye to her parents, family, garden, neighbors, and friends, and asks for forgiveness if she has ever hurt them by word or deed. This is a rather sorrowful part of the celebration, accompanied by the bride's family's *raudos* (RAO-dohs), or farewell songs.

Parents prepare dowry chests for their daughters well in advance. These chests are made from the wood of a tree in which storks nest, so as to bring luck and fertility. The chests are filled with jewelry, documents, letters, money, a rue wreath, medicinal herbs, clothes for the firstborn child, linens, bedclothes, rolls of fabric, woven sashes, and other handmade articles. The size and beauty of her dowry chest is an indication of the bride's wealth, status, taste, and industry.

HEALTH

Until 1940, health care was provided by both state and private facilities. The Soviets introduced comprehensive state-funded health care. After Lithuania's independence in 1991, a National Health Concept was adopted that shed the Soviet system and called for extensive reforms. The 1992 constitution guarantees the right of all citizens to receive old-age pensions, disability pensions, and assistance in the event of unemployment, sickness, or widowhood. Since 1997, a compulsory national health-care insurance plan covers all residents.

There are about 4.12 doctors and 7 hospital beds for every 1,000 people in Lithuania, as compared with about 2.45 doctors and 2.9 hospital beds for every 1,000 people in the United States. Doctors are well trained, but they are forced to work with limited supplies of medical instruments, materials, and medicines.

The infant mortality rate is 3.8 deaths per 1,000 live births (in 2016). For comparison, the infant mortality rate in the United States is 5.8 deaths per 1,000 live births, while in Russia, the rate is 6.9 per 1,000. Infant mortality rate is one indicator of a nation's general health and well being. Another is

A man and his granddaughter feed pigeons in a city park in Vilnius.

life expectancy at birth. In Lithuania in 2016, that statistic was an average of 74.9 years for the total population. A baby boy born in Lithuania in 2016 could expect to live to age 69.5 years, while a baby girl could expect to live to age 80.6 years. Again, for comparison, a baby born that same year in the United States could expect to live to age 79.8 on average (77.5 for males, 82.1 for females).

THE ELDERLY

Great respect is given to elders in Lithuanian society. A younger person would respectfully address an elderly person as grandmother, grandfather, uncle, or aunty, never by his or her name.

In modern Lithuania, where both parents work, grandparents often take care of their grandchildren. In fact, they may move in with their children and grandchildren. This gives the grandmother and grandfather an opportunity to teach the third generation about Lithuanian customs, beliefs, traditions, folktales, crafts, games, dances, and music, and to retell stories of their ancient heritage and mythology. Nursing homes are rare in Lithuania.

FUNERALS

In villages, the dead lie in state at home for three days. In towns and cities, they lie in the funeral parlor for two days. The footpath in front of the house or funeral parlor is strewn with pieces of spruce branches.

The dead person is dressed in his or her best clothes and laid in a coffin, which is placed in a room with beautiful woven bedspreads fixed on the walls. A cross, some pictures of saints, and two burning candles are placed at the head. Wreaths and ribbons inscribed with words of condolence are also hung on the walls or placed on the sides of the coffin.

Family and friends keep vigil throughout the days and nights. Silence is observed as much as possible, as it is thought that though the spirit separates from the body at death, it does not leave the house until the deceased is carried away. In the evenings the neighbors gather to pray and sing hymns written by local poets. After the prayers, a funerary meal is served. If the family owns a pig, it is butchered for this meal.

In southeastern Lithuania, the tradition of *raudos* at funerals still survives. Laments, spoken or sung by professionals or relatives, express the sorrow of the living and the sad plight of the children left behind, as well as recalling the good deeds of the deceased.

In the country, the dead are usually buried in the morning. Before closing the lid, a cross is burned onto the lid with a hallowed candle. It is traditional to give the dead person a last kiss. After the coffin is lowered into the grave, everyone there throws in a handful of earth. Throwing flowers into the grave is a new gesture. After burial, a cross is pressed onto the top of the mound and wreaths and flowers are laid on it.

INTERNET LINKS

https://www.numbeo.com/cost-of-living/country_result. jsp?country=Lithuania&displayCurrency=USD
See the up-to-date, average prices of everyday expenses in Lithuania, listed in US dollars, on this site.

http://www.truelithuania.com/topics/history-and-politics-of-lithuania/society
This site presents a broad picture of Lithuanian society and covers a variety of lifestyle topics.

RELIGION

The Hill of Crosses in Šiauliai is an important pilgrimage site in the Baltic region.

8

THE LITHUANIANS WERE THE last Europeans to relinquish their ancient beliefs and rites. The country converted to Christianity only in the fourteenth century. Today the main religion of Lithuania is Roman Catholicism. While most ethnic Lithuanians and virtually all Poles are Roman Catholics, there are also small pockets of Lutherans, Calvinists, and some other Protestant denominations. Adherents of Russian Orthodoxy and the Old Believers (Old Ritualists) are mostly Russians. There are some Tatars, who are Muslim, and a small Jewish community.

PRE-CHRISTIAN RELIGION

The religion of the ancient Lithuanians was based on animism—the belief that all things have a spirit. Ancient Lithuanians worshipped objects and natural phenomena. Cults devoted to forests and fires were widespread. There were sacred fields and forests that no one was allowed to enter or work in. Certain kinds of trees, such as oaks and pines, held special powers. As late as the eighteenth century, Catholic officials were still

A neo-pagan group called Romuva is one of Lithuania's fastest growing religious communities. Followers are attempting to rediscover and restore pre-Christian beliefs, which they feel are a more authentic reflection of Lithuanian heritage. With members making up some 0.2 percent of the population, neo-paganism is now the country's sixth-largest faith.

chopping down sacred oak trees in an attempt to suppress Lithuanians' pagan beliefs. Lithuanians have retained a reverence for nature and a belief in the sanctity of all living things, and elements of the ancient religion survive to this day through legends, folktales, exorcisms, and songs.

The prehistoric hunters and farmers of Lithuania had a matriarchal tribal system, and their religious imagery was female. The later patriarchal tribal and feudal systems enabled the introduction of male gods and saw the decline of the importance of goddesses, although some goddesses remained in the Lithuanian pantheon of gods side-by-side with male deities.

Places of worship were outdoors, usually in a sacred grove of trees, on a hillside, or near a holy stream. There were special people, usually men, who performed religious rituals. These men, similar to priests, were the wise men and leaders of a community. The sacrifice of animals— calves, pigs, sheep, goats, and chickens—was common and continued into the 1500s. Human sacrifice was not practiced except after a victorious battle, when the commander of the enemy forces would be sacrificed to thank the gods.

Wooden replicas of pagan idols stand at the top of Birute Hill in Žemaičių Alka Šventojoje, where an ancient astronomical observatory has been reconstructed.

CHRISTIANITY'S RUGGED ROAD

Christian teachings first reached Lithuania in the eleventh and twelfth centuries, but it took a long while before they were accepted. In 1251, Mindaugas adopted Christianity in his bid to have Pope Innocent crown him king, hoping to avoid attacks by Christian warriors. Soon after, though, he reverted to his old ways and sacrificed a Christian princess to Perkunas, the god of thunder. A later attempt to introduce Catholicism was more successful: Grand Duke Jogaila converted to Roman Catholicism and made it the religion of his country in 1385 when he married Princess Jadwiga of Poland.

It was a difficult beginning, though. The first Christian church in Lithuania was built near Kaunas. It had a roof that sloped steeply. According to legend,

The ancient Lithuanian religion was polytheistic, meaning that many gods were worshipped. The pantheon of Lithuanian gods was rich and diverse. The god of bright daylight, Dievas, the supreme deity, was a kind, gentle, and wise god. The most popular god was Perkunas, the god of thunder. He was master of the atmosphere and the "waters" of the sky, as well as fertility, human morality, and justice. Under the influence of Christianity, Perkunas was transformed into the Lord of Heaven. Velnias was the guardian of wizards and sages. The goddess of forests was Medeina, and Zvorune was the goddess of hunting. There were female deities representing the sun, the moon, water, earth, and fertility. Other goddesses were responsible for the birth, life, and death of man, flora, and fauna. These deities took care that the continuity of life in the world was maintained through the perpetual ebb and flow of life and death.

the roof had not sloped when it was constructed. The god Perkunas so mightily resented the presence of a Christian church that he engulfed it in a storm, which caused the church building to sink and so increased the slope of the roof.

Protestantism—first Lutheranism and then Calvinism—came to Lithuania in the sixteenth century. In the seventeenth century, largely due to the efforts of the Jesuits, Lithuania was reclaimed by the Roman Catholics. At that time, a number of Old Believers (the Old Ritualists) settled in Lithuania, having fled from Russia to avoid persecution. Catholicism flourished in the seventeenth and eighteenth centuries. Many churches and monasteries were built, and the ranks of priests grew.

In 1795, however, a greater part of Lithuania was annexed to Russia, and the dominion of the Roman Catholic Church was restricted. In the nineteenth century the Catholic Church was persecuted. Monasteries were shut down and churches were given over to the Russian Orthodox Church. From 1799 to 1915, the Russian Orthodox faith was the official religion in Lithuania, although the Lithuanians tried to remain Catholic. The most prominent figure

St. Anne's Church in Vilnius, dating to 1500, is a UNESCO World Heritage site.

in the struggle to uphold the Lithuanian cultural identity was Bishop Motiejus Valancius. In time, the Russian authorities relented, and in 1897 the ban on building Catholic churches was lifted.

Under the Lithuanian Republic (1918—1940), the Roman Catholic Church regained its place as the official religion of the state. Direct ties with the Vatican were established in 1922. The Lithuanian Church Province was created in 1926 under direct subordination to the pope, and relations with the Vatican were stabilized in 1927. The state also supported other religious communities, including other Christians as well as Muslims and Jews.

SOVIET REPRESSION

Lithuania's incorporation into the Soviet Union in June 1940 caused major losses to all churches, including, to a lesser degree, the Russian Orthodox Church and the Old Believers. All the Catholic monasteries and 690 churches were shut down, and church lands were confiscated by the state. Many surrendered churches became concert halls or museums—Saint Casimir's, in Vilnius, was turned into a Museum of Atheism. Religious literature was suppressed, and religious instruction banned. Those who attended church could find their careers in jeopardy, and their children would be excluded from higher education.

In this atmosphere of repression, religious practices were carried on secretly. For example, a group of Catholic priests regularly published the *Chronicles of the Lithuanian Catholic Church*, which informed the world about local repression and human rights violations.

The persecution of the churches came to an end in 1988. In 1990, the Act of the Restitution of the Catholic Church was proclaimed, bringing freedom of worship once more to all Lithuanians. Today about 77.2 percent of Lithuanians are Roman Catholic. Monasteries and convents have reopened, and workers are renovating churches. In 1989, the Catholic organization Caritas, the Lithuanian Catholic Teachers' Union, and the Catholic Action Center resumed their activities. In 1990, the Lithuanian Catholic Academy of Sciences was moved back to Lithuania from abroad.

St. Casimir Church in Vilnius, from 1618, is the oldest Baroque-style church in the city.

RUSSIAN ORTHODOX CHURCH

In 1054, Christianity underwent a major east-west division. The outcome resulted in the Roman Catholic Church and the Greek Orthodox Church, which later migrated to Russia. The name of the church in Russia is the Russian Orthodox Church. The church is headed by the Patriarch of All Russia and does not recognize the pope as the head of the Church. Members of the Orthodox Church in Lithuania are almost exclusively Russians or other Slavs. Some 4 percent of the population are followers of this faith. There are fewer than one hundred small parishes and congregations, governed by city and national church bodies, under the jurisdiction of the patriarchate in Moscow.

CROSSES AND MINIATURE CHAPELS

As Christianity is the dominant religion in Lithuania, the image of the cross plays an important role in the life of Lithuanians. Many crosses and miniature chapels are found on posts along roadsides, in yards and on homes, on farmsteads, in graveyards, on hill slopes and hilltops, beside rivers and springs, near forests, and in town squares. Some crosses incorporate pre-Christian religious elements, such as the sun, moon, and serpents. The crosses in Lithuania can be divided into two broad types: the pillar type, which has a concealed and scarcely noticeable crossbeam, and the more recognizable T-shaped cross.

Crosses are built for various purposes. Some are erected in cemeteries and in places where accidents have occurred in remembrance of the dead. They are put up in villages, fields, and along roads in the hope that God will give blessings, grant a good harvest, and keep away epidemics, droughts, quarrels, and other misfortunes. Other occasions for installing crosses include moving to a new home or farm, births, christenings, weddings, and times of success or misfortune in the family.

Miniature chapels are suspended from trees, nailed to homes, mounted on niches cut in tree trunks, or mounted on poles in fields and forests. Some are simple and others ornate. They are like miniature houses or little chapels showing a statue or statues within. In some areas it is customary to affix a chapel to a tree when there is a birth or a death in the family.

Crosses and miniature chapels are found at places that are believed to be haunted and at springs whose waters are thought to have healing powers. Miniature chapels dedicated to Saint John the Baptist are erected near rivers and bridges. Village communities, small towns, religious fraternities, and youth organizations each have their own cross.

The variety of crosses is evident in the exceptionally rich ornamentation and mix of materials. Huge crosses, some reaching 10 feet (3 m) in height, are carved out of stone. Wooden crosses and miniature chapels have ornate iron decorations that incorporate smaller crosses, trumpeting angels, and other Christian symbols into designs of radiating wavy sunbeams, arrows, crescents, stylized pine trees, lilies, and tulips.

The best example of Lithuanian crosses is the Hill of Crosses, just north of Šiauliai, where thousands of crosses are mounted on a hill. The hill is not as tall as it once was. It was bulldozed by the Soviets three times, and each time new crosses would be brought to replace the demolished ones.

THE OLD BELIEVERS

About 0.8 percent of Lithuanians are Old Believers, also called Old Ritualists. These congregations are headed by the Supreme Pomorski Old Ritualists' Council in Vilnius. The Old Believers is a group that formed as the result of a schism in the Russian Orthodox Church in the seventeenth century. Many adherents emigrated to the Baltic states to avoid religious persecution. They have no hierarchy, no priests, and no sacraments except baptism. Since 1971, they have been officially recognized by the council of the Russian Orthodox Church. Nevertheless, many Old Believer communities are somewhat secretive and keep themselves apart from other groups, sometimes even other Old Believer congregations.

OTHER CHRISTIAN DENOMINATIONS

The Evangelical Lutheran Church in Marijampolė was built in the early 1800s by Germans who had moved to the region.

Lutheranism came to Lithuania in the early 1500s. Today about 0.6 percent of people are members of the Lutheran Church there. The Lutheran congregations are governed by the Consistory of the Evangelical Lutheran Church of Lithuania in Taurage, which has been a member of the Lutheran World Foundation since 1968. Together with the Reformed Evangelical Church, it publishes the periodical *Lietuvosevangelikukelias* (*The Road of the Lithuanian Evangelicals*).

Other very small Christian denominations in Lithuania include the Reformed Evangelical Church, the Evangelical Baptists, the Evangelical Faith in the Spirit of Apostles, the Seventh-day Adventists, Calvinists, and the Eastern Rites Roman Catholics. The Lutherans, Calvinists, and Evangelists are most heavily concentrated in the coastal region, mainly because of the strong German influence in that area.

ISLAM

Islam came to Lithuania in the fourteenth century from the Crimea and Kazan, a town on the Volga River, through the Tatars.

For the last six centuries, the Tatars of Lithuania have maintained their ethnic identity as well as their religion. They live primarily in compact communities where the mosque is the central focus of their lives.

There were altogether forty-eight mosques in the grand duchy of Lithuania from 1397 to the end of the eighteenth century. During the commemoration in 1930 of the five hundredth anniversary of Vytautas the Great's death, the government of Lithuania built a mosque in Kaunas in recognition of the Tatars.

During the fifty years of Soviet occupation, Lithuanian Muslims, like other ethnic religious groups, were prevented from practicing their faith. Now about 3,200 Tatars live in Lithuania, making up most of the Muslim community. There are five major congregations of Muslims in Lithuania, and they worship at the Raiziai Mosque in Alytus (built in the late nineteenth century), the Vytautas Didysis Mosque at Kaunas (1930), the Nemezis Mosque (early twentieth century), and the oldest existing mosque, which is in the village of Keturiasdesimt Totoriu (1815). The lifting of religious repression since independence has cleared the way for new mosques to be built. The Tatar community is now trying to rebuild the Lukiskes Mosque in Vilnius, destroyed during the Soviet occupation.

INTERNET LINKS

http://www.hillofcrosses.com
The site of the Hill of Crosses in Siauliai has photos of this unusual place.

http://www.truelithuania.com/topics/culture-of-lithuania/religions-faiths-in-lithuania
A good overview of religions and churches in Lithuania is available on this site.

LANGUAGE

Civic signage in Lithuanian language forbids certain activities on Gediminas Avenue in Vilnius.

9

LANGUAGES ARE A BIT LIKE DNA. They are markers of a people's origins, passed along through the generations, acquiring mutations and variations along the way. Even as they may change and evolve, however, languages retain the linguistic genetic codes, so to speak, of a population's history.

The Lithuanian word *aciu*, meaning "thank you," sounds like the English sneeze word, "achoo!"

A man reads a newspaper in park in Birstonas.

A customer makes a purchase at a Lietuvos Spauda newspaper kiosk in Vilnius. Lietuvos Spauda is Lithuania's largest network of newstands.

The Lithuanian language is particularly revealing in that way. It's the oldest living language in Europe today and retains many archaic features. Lithuanian is more ancient than Greek, Latin, German, Celtic, or the Slav tongues—some linguistic historians say Lithuanian is the most ancient of all the living languages.

THE LITHUANIAN LANGUAGE

The Lithuanian language belongs to the Baltic branch of the great Indo-European family. It is related to most of the other languages of Europe and Western Asia, from India to Iceland. Its ultimate source is the extinct language of India called Sanskrit. The early Indo-European languages were spoken five thousand years ago by people who settled in Ukraine, southern Russia, the Euphrates, the Rhine and Indus valleys, and around the Aral Sea.

The Baltic branch consists of Lithuanian, Latvian, the extinct Old Prussian language, and the extinct dialects of the Curonians, Semigallians, and

The Lithuanian language uses the Latin alphabet. There are thirty-two letters in the alphabet. Unique Lithuanian sounds are represented by special characters.

Vowels:

a – as in ah	*e – as in there*	*ė – as in make*	*i – as in sit*
o – as in shot	*u – as in should*	*ū – oo as in truth*	*y – ee as in see*

ą, ę, į, ų appear in special cases and are pronounced a bit longer.

Consonants:

b, d, f, g, h, k, l, m, n, p, t, and v are pronounced almost as in English

c – ts as in tickets	*č – ch as in chin*	*s – as in sit*	*š – sh as in she*
z – as in zoo	*ž – as in vision*	*j – y as in yes*	*r – is always trilled*

Selonians. The Lithuanian and Latvian languages separated during the fifth to seventh centuries CE, with Lithuanian retaining more ancient features than Latvian.

Of all the living languages in Europe today, Lithuanian is the most archaic and has most faithfully preserved the primitive features of Sanskrit. This has happened because Lithuanian was spoken by a people whose environment isolated them for many centuries from the outside world by dense forests and impassable marshes.

A very great many Lithuanian words are used by Belorussians and Poles in the areas formerly inhabited by Lithuanians. A complete dictionary of the Lithuanian language consists of twenty volumes, containing about four hundred thousand entries.

During the Soviet era, Russian increasingly displaced Lithuanian in the country's cultural, economic, administrative, and political life. Major government institutions operated entirely in Russian. In 1989, the government reinstated Lithuanian as the national language.

Lithuanian is spoken by some three million people in Lithuania and by another one million living abroad. Lithuania is also rich in dialects and regional accents. The two principal dialects are Aukštaitian (Highland Lithuanian) and Samogitian (Lowland Lithuanian). Standard Lithuanian is based on Western Aukštaitian. Other languages spoken in Lithuania include Russian (as the second language), Latvian, Polish, and Belorussian. The languages of commerce and business are English, German, and French, with English slowly gaining popularity as the favored second language.

LITHUANIAN WISDOM AND ADVICE

Every nation has its treasury of proverbs, brief and popular statements of wisdom or advice. Called *patarle* (PAH-tehr-lay) in Lithuanian, proverbs are easy to remember.

In traveling globally by word of mouth from person to person, proverbs often retain their deeper meaning but change in their manner of expression

People peruse the offerings at an indoor book market in Vilnius.

according to local circumstances. Therefore the English proverb "A bird in the hand is worth two in the bush" appears in Lithuanian as "A sparrow in the hand is better than an elk in the woods" and "A sparrow in the palm is better than a crane on the roof."

Sometimes Lithuanians translate proverbs literally, such as the Sanskrit proverb "God has given teeth, God will give bread." At other times they express ideas in their own way—the English proverb "You can't get blood out of a stone" becomes "You can't shatter a wall with your head."

How would you describe a gluttonous and lazy person? Lithuanians would say he or she "eats like a horse and works like a rooster." How about a man who is happy for no reason? He would be said to be "as happy as though he has found a bit of iron." Such Lithuanian sayings and maxims are full of humor and are used as tools to educate children. Looking for something? "Maybe you'll find it in the dew!"

STORYTELLING

At parties and gatherings, storytelling is a popular form of entertainment. Popular legends, dating from pre-Christian times, are inhabited by devils, sorcerers, ghosts, and spirits. According to these tales, people traveling in remote places and at odd hours might just encounter such creatures, for better or for worse.

Short stories without endings and tales about animals are especially popular among children. Domestic and forest animals that behave like human beings inhabit these stories. Heroes are often aided by magical objects and heavenly or earthly helpers. There are also modern stories about clever hired hands, gullible landlords, and matchmakers. Often, stories are embellished with short, simple songs, as if a character in the story were singing it.

Mystical stories are common and are often the most artful. In these tales, heroes battle dragons or free people who have been turned into swans or other beings. The tragic story of Žilvinas, the king of the grass snakes, his wife Egle, and their family is a relic of the ancient cult of the grass snake.

EGLĖ, QUEEN OF THE GRASS SNAKES

Once upon a time there was an old man and an old woman. They had twelve sons and three daughters. The youngest daughter's name was Eglė (AG-lay), and she was the darling of the family. One summer evening she went for a swim in the sea. When she finished her swim and wanted to change back into her clothes, she found a grass snake lying curled in her shirtsleeve. He said he would give her shirt back if she agreed to marry him. So Eglė promised to marry him.

In a few days, she left her parents' house escorted by a retinue of grass snakes. On the shore of the sea she was met by a handsome young man who was actually the grass snake that had curled up in her shirtsleeve. They crossed in a boat to an island nearby, and from there they descended into a beautiful palace at the bottom of the sea where they celebrated their wedding. Life in the palace was blissful. Eglė forgot her homeland altogether, for she was happy. She gave birth to three sons—Ąžuolas (Oak), Uosis (Ash), and Berzas (Birch)—and last, a daughter, Drebulė (Poplar).

Nine years passed. Her oldest son asked her where her parents were and said he would like to visit them. Eglė remembered her family again and wanted to go to see them, but her husband, Žilvinas, would not let her go because he was afraid she would not come back. He asked her to finish three tasks before she would be allowed to go.

The first task was to spin a bundle of silk. Eglė spun and spun, but no matter how fast she worked, the bundle stayed the same size, so she asked a wise old woman for advice. The woman told her to throw the bundle into the fire. The unspun silk burned away to reveal a toad that had been producing new silk as Eglė spun. Her second task was to wear down iron shoes. Eglė accomplished this task also with the advice of the old woman, who told her to go to a foundry and ask the blacksmith to burn them down. Her third task was to bake a pie with just a sieve for a tool. But Žilvinas had given orders to hide all the water-holding and cooking vessels in the kingdom. Eglė could not even fetch water for the pie. On the advice of the old woman, she filled the holes of the sieve with bread dough, let it dry, and then brought some water from the river in it and made the pie.

Having accomplished all three tasks, she said good-bye to her husband on the seashore and, together with her children, departed for her parents' house. Before parting, Eglė agreed that when she came back she would call her husband out of the sea by saying "Žilvinas, Žilvinas, if alive you are, milk white is the surf! If dead you are, blood red is the surf!"

Eglė and her children had a very good time with her parents and siblings. When the time allotted for the visit was drawing to a close, Eglė's brothers were unhappy and tried to get the password from her sons, so they could go and kill Žilvinas. Try as they would, they could not get it out of her sons. But the daughter, Drebulė, blurted it out when her uncles threatened to flog her.

When Eglė and her children came back to the seashore and tried to call Žilvinas, they found the roiling surf breaking blood red on the shore, and heard Žilvinas's voice coming from the bottom of the sea telling them of the betrayal. In her grief and pain, Eglė gathered her children and said, "My brave sons, because of your courage and fortitude, you shall stand as the strongest of trees for all the day. But, you, my daughter, shall tremble at the slightest breeze and the rains shall ever wash your mouth." She then turned her sons into strong trees—oak, ash, and birch, and her daughter into the quivering poplar. She herself turned into an evergreen fir.

INTERNET LINKS

http://www.omniglot.com/writing/lithuanian.htm
Omniglot provides a good introduction to the Lithuanian language.

http://www.truelithuania.com/lithuanian-mythology-and-folklore-3474
Lithuanian folklore is introduced on this site, with a photo of a sculpture of the character Eglė.

ARTS

A curious monument to the American rock musician
Frank Zappa stands in Vilnius.

10

LITHUANIA IS MUSIC—FROM ITS popular jazz, pop, and rock festivals to classic opera and symphonic orchestras to its beloved folk music choirs and traditional instrument ensembles. Lithuania is museum-worthy modern art and roadside folk carvings and household crafts. It is a literature of Soviet occupation and oppression, a literature of exile, and of independence. And it is a culture rich with a deep history of mythology and legend.

In Vilnius and other major cities, the arts and culture scene is lively. Theaters, concert halls, museums, and exhibition halls are open year-round. During the summer months, many cultural festivals and drama and music competitions are held. There are many professional theaters, some state orchestras, and chamber groups in the major cities. Lithuania also has as more than fifty museums, such as the Mykolas Zilinskas gallery in Kaunas, holding significant collections of artworks.

THEATER AND BALLET

Lithuania has a very long history of performance art, arising from ancient rituals and entertainments.

During the Soviet era, several Lithuanian plays were banned, and the theater had to extol the virtues of Communism. Now that Lithuania

A bust of the eccentric American rock musician Frank Zappa (1940-1993) stands incongruously in a court yard in Vilnius. Created by Lithuanian sculptor Konstantinas Bogdanas in 1995, it's the only public statue of Zappa in the world. Oddly, Zappa had no connection to Lithuania, but he was a cult favorite of the country's pro-independence artists and intellectuals. The Vilnius Zappa sculpture is now a tourist attraction.

The Lithuanian National Opera and Ballet Theater.

is independent again, the theater enjoys much more freedom. In Vilnius, there are thirteen professional theaters and a number of concert halls. Kaunas has a branch of the National Philharmonic Orchestra, a pantomime theater school, a puppet theater, and a youth chamber music theater. The Lithuanian Theater of Youth is popular locally and is known abroad.

Lithuanian ballet has a reputation of high professional quality. At the outset of World War II, many fine dancers fled the country. After the war, however, the Academic Opera and Ballet Theater revived and continued to operate in Vilnius even throughout the Soviet years. It performed several Lithuanian pieces, and elements of folk dancing were skillfully worked into its repertoire. In 2015, the ballet company celebrated its ninetieth anniversary.

MUSIC

The Baltic States are famous for their choral singing. So far, about five hundred thousand Lithuanian folk songs have been collated, including songs about work, love, war, and motherhood. There are many professional and amateur choirs in Lithuania. Every five years there is a huge song festival called Dainų Šventė, where choirs, folk dance ensembles, and folk orchestras come from all over Lithuania to perform. Choir members number in the thousands and the audiences attend in the tens or even hundreds of thousands—a large proportion of the population. There are also smaller song and dance festivals throughout the year. Under Soviet rule, these festivals were among the very few ways in which national feeling could be legally expressed, although several of the more ardent patriotic songs were banned. The song festivals became a vehicle for nationalist sentiment, and the independence movement in the Baltic States has often been called the Singing Revolution.

Lithuania has produced several notable composers, including M. K. Ciurlionis (1875—1911) and modernist Osvaldas Balakauskas (b. 1937), who is currently head of the Composition Department of the Lithuanian Academy of Music and Theatre. His works include symphonies, concertos, and chamber music. In 1996, he was awarded with the Lithuanian National Award, the highest artistic and cultural distinction in Lithuania. The following year, that award was given to Onutė Narbutaitė (b. 1956), perhaps the most famous Lithuanian composer working today. Her works have been performed in concerts and festivals worldwide.

The National Philharmonic building in Vilnius houses the symphony orchestra and is also an umbrella organization for many other musical groups and soloists. There is an active live music scene, with bands performing rock, alternative music, and jazz throughout the land.

The Lithuania National Philharmonic Society building in Vilnius.

Artists played an important leadership role in the Baltic independence movement. In Lithuania, a music professor, Vytautas Landsbergis, became the country's leader in 1990. Popular culture—particularly rock music, which was banned under Soviet rule—united many sections of the population and was used to express defiance during the 1980s. The most influential rock group in the 1980s was Foje, whose gloomy lyrics were reflective of life under Soviet rule. Although rock music today has not reached the dizzying heights it did two decades ago, it is still as popular. This is evident in the increase in the number of rock festivals in major cities.

FOLK ART

Lithuanian folk art embraces a great variety of forms from graphic art, religious art, and primitive painting to woodcarving, textiles, ceramics, and blacksmithing. Folk craft festivals and displays are a popular feature of Lithuania's cultural life.

The southwestern region of Lithuania is the home of kankles *(KAHN-klis) music. The kankles is one of the most ancient stringed instruments in the Baltic countries. It had been on the verge of extinction, but was revived by a few enthusiasts just before World War II. Looking something like a handheld harp, the kankles is a kind of board zither with between five and twelve iron or natural fiber strings. It goes back at least three thousand years and is native to the Baltic region. The word kankles means "the singing tree" and comes from the Indo-European word* qan, *meaning "to sing" or "sound."*

Kankles are thought to be associated with death. Lithuanians believe that in order to make sonorous kankles, the wood from which they are crafted has to be cut from a mature forest on the day that a loved one dies. As the household

mourns, the wood acquires depth and soul. It is shaped like a small boat or coffin. Kankles are made by skilled master craftsmen and are not easy to find. There are also few musicians who know how to play the instrument, although a folk revival in the 1970s and 1980s has revived interest in traditional instruments. The most famous kankles player in Lithuania is Lina Naikelienė. Her Kankles Ensemble Trio has played worldwide. Playing the kankles is said to be much like meditating and is thought to protect the musician from disease, accidents, and death.

Lithuania has an especially rich tradition of woodcarving. One ancient craft was the carving of ritual wooden masks. These carvings have preserved some elements of ancient sorcery practices. Their most distinctive feature is folk humor and satire. Wooden crosses are another important folk art. They are often covered with ancient pre-Christian symbols. A more modern example of Lithuanian woodcarving skill is the group of wooden memorial sculptures commemorating the residents of the village of Ablinga, which was burned together with all its inhabitants by the Nazis. In the field where Ablinga once stood, about 25 miles (40 km) from Klaipėda, large wooden sculptures have been erected for the families of the dead. Sculptures made from flax and straw are also popular. Elaborate sculptures like the "wedding gardens" are particularly enjoyed in Aukštaitija. Other well-known examples of folk arts can be seen at the Witches' Hill in Juodkrantė and at the Hill of Crosses near Šiauliai.

Wood folk sculptures populate the forest in Witches' Hill Park in Juodkrantė.

M. K. ČIURLIONIS

Mikalojus Konstantinas Čiurlionis (1875–1911) was born in the Dzūkija region. Before he died, at the early age of thirty-six, he almost single-handedly founded modern Lithuanian culture through his work as a painter, composer, and organizer of cultural events.

Both in painting and music, Ciurlionis was a pioneer and

The Fairy Tale Castle (1909), by M. K. Ciurlionis

founder of new forms. He composed many works that are still performed, including the first Lithuanian symphony, In the Forest.

After establishing himself as a composer, Ciurlionis took up painting, believing that there were certain emotions that were better expressed in shapes and colors than in music. In his painting he created a mystical universe with motifs from Lithuanian folklore. He was among those who initiated the annual Lithuanian Art Exhibition in Vilnius in 1907.

PETRAS KALPOKAS *(1880–1945) The works of this Lithuanian artist belong to the period of the formation of Lithuania's national fine arts awareness. He took deep interest in the first Lithuanian Art Exhibition in 1907 and was an active participant in other art exhibitions. He engaged in various fields of art, producing paintings, frescos, and cartoons. His major works, however, were landscape and portrait paintings. He taught painting at the Kaunas School of Art and at the Institute of Decorative and Applied Arts.*

LITERATURE

Lithuania's first pieces of writing date back to the Middle Ages. They were not written in Lithuanian, however, but in Old Church Slavic, Latin, and Polish.

The first book in the Lithuanian language, the Protestant Catechism, was printed in 1547. The Lithuanian text, in Gothic letters, is often uneven and not clearly printed. When out of one type, the printer simply substituted it with another. Between two hundred and three hundred copies were printed. Only two copies remain today—one in the library of Vilnius University and the other in the library of Torun University, Poland.

During the next two centuries, more religious texts in the local language appeared as more people learned to read. This laid the foundation for Lithuania's literary language.

Several Lithuanian writers wrote patriotic ballads and prose during the eighteenth century Russian occupation. In 1864 the Russian czar banned the printing of Lithuanian works. Poetic literature flourished across the border in Prussia, however, where the Lithuanian poet Maironis lived, and in the émigré community in the United States. Maironis was a leader in glorifying all things Lithuanian. His verses are still read, and his poems have been translated into English. Some of the leading poets of the period include Vilius Vydunas, Juozas Tumas-Vaižgantas, and Antanas Vienuolis. Prose writing developed after the ban was lifted in 1904.

Independence in 1918 ushered in a new era of creativity. Vincas Mykolaitis-Putinas wrote *Altoriu Sesely*, one of Lithuania's major novels. Women writers, such as Žemait (Julija Zymantiene), Sofija Kymantaitė-Čiurlionienė, and the poet Salomėja Nėris, flourished.

Although some good prose and poetry were produced during the Soviet era, the repression stifled literary development overall. Often the writings in the 1990s reflect the writers' experience of the Soviet occupation, and many express a dark, cynical, and sad tone. Popular writers include Juozas Aputis, Vytautas Bubnys, and Vytautas Martinkus. The novels of Bubnys and Martinkus show the continuing attraction of folk themes.

Two internationally known contemporary writers of the Lithuanian language are the poet and essayist Tomas Venclova, who won the

Lithuanian National Prize in 2000, and satirist and children's author Vytautė Žilinskaitė. In 2007, she was awarded the Children's Literature Prize by the Lithuanian Minister of Education and Science. The Lithuanian Writers' Union also helped advance the literary scene by offering contemporary Lithuanian poetry and prose in its English language magazine, *Vilnius*.

ARCHITECTURE

Lithuania's rural architecture expresses the people's farming background and lifestyle. Timber is by far the most common building material. The earliest houses had thatched roofs; later, wood shingles, clay, and tin were used. Some buildings have ornately carved woodwork. The skills of building are passed along from generation to generation with few changes introduced along the way. The oldest standing wooden houses date back to the eighteenth century.

City architecture—fortifications and churches—was of stone, and it is these buildings that give the old cities their stable atmosphere today. Other buildings were made of wood until the nineteenth century.

Architectural styles followed those of Western Europe. Early Gothic structures in Lithuania were heavy, massive buildings with thick walls, small windows, and huge, imposing buttresses. Examples of typical early Gothic architecture in the country are Saint Michael's Church in Vilnius, built at the end of the fourteenth century, and Saint Michael's Church in Kaunas. Late Gothic churches of the fifteenth and sixteenth centuries are much larger and lighter structures. The best example of this progression is Saint Anne's Church in Vilnius.

The high baroque period produced the Church of Saints Peter and Paul in Vilnius and the church and convent of the Sisters of Saint Casimir at Pazaislis near Kaunas. The convent is hexagonal and had a great copper roof. Over the centuries it has suffered from the vandalism and looting of invading armies.

In the late eighteenth century, classicism and romanticism became the predominant architectural styles. Towns followed a rectangular grid. During the nineteenth century many of the cities' wooden buildings were replaced with stone structures.

After independence in 1918, an intensive growth of towns began. The countryside changed radically as the land was divided into individual holdings spreading all over the country. Rural architecture continued to maintain the traditions of Lithuanian folk architecture.

Architecture took a step backward during the Soviet era. Huge, drab, cheaply-built high-rises and housing projects were the buildings of the day. Many are already dilapidated. Today, the restoration of these existing buildings takes precedence over undertaking any brand-new housing projects.

INTERNET LINKS

http://www.atlasobscura.com/places/hill-of-witches
The Atlas Obscura site presents a page dedicated to Lithuania's Hill of Witches, with images of its wooden folk art.

https://www.mcsweeneys.net/articles/in-search-of-frank-zappa-vilnius-lithuania
This intriguing article recalls the author's visit to Vilnius, and his search for the infamous Frank Zappa statue.

http://www.opera.lt/en
All content on the informative Lithuanian National Opera and Ballet Theater site is available in English.

https://theculturetrip.com/europe/lithuania/articles/10-lithuanian-artists-and-writers-you-should-know
This page discusses some of Lithuania's most influential artists and writers.

http://www.truelithuania.com/topics/culture-of-lithuania/architecture-of-lithuania
This site offers several pages about various historical movements in architecture in Lithuania, with photos.

LEISURE

Old men play chess in Bernadine Park in Vilnius.

WINTERS ARE LONG AND COLD, and summers are very short in Lithuania. During the winter months, indoor leisure activities are popular, especially storytelling by grandparents. Woodcarving and handicrafts created from flax and fibers are old traditions for occupying the short winter days, as is singing and playing of musical instruments. Other pastimes popular in the winter are skiing and ice skating.

During the summer, Lithuanians make the most of the warm weather. Forests, rivers, and lakes are within easy reach of city and country alike. In June, when the school term ends, many children are sent to stay with relatives in the country for the entire three-month vacation. Their mothers may accompany them, and fathers visit on weekends.

In the country there is less leisure time than in the city. Leisure time is generally used for handicrafts. Women's and girls' hobbies include drawing, knitting, crocheting, and sash weaving. These skills are passed down from mother to daughter. There are also get-togethers for name days and other church and traditional holidays, weddings, christenings, funerals, and even for the slaughter of an animal, when neighbors and relatives are invited for a feast.

11

The Snow Arena in Druskininkai, Lithuania, completed in 2011, has one of the world's largest indoor ski slopes. It measures 1509 feet (460 m) long, 207 feet (63 m) wide, and 213 feet (66 m) high. The indoor site also has a terrain park for extreme sports lovers, a beginner's slope, and even a chair lift—as well as restaurants and bars.

Young people from the country go to nearby towns to see plays, visit dance clubs, or play sports. The most popular sport in Lithuania is basketball. In bad weather, young city people gather in cafés to talk, listen to music, use the Internet, and drink coffee. Most cafés also serve alcohol. Vilnius specializes in beer bars, which are often cavernous cellars.

SINGING

Singing is a way of life in Lithuania. Family get-togethers are occasions to sit and sing songs of their ancient land, mythology, customs, and folklore. Lithuanians are good at improvisation, and like to make up lullabies.

People young and old join song and dance groups, traditional country bands, or pop groups to occupy their leisure hours. The many music festivals held throughout Lithuania are testament to the people's love of singing. Some of the songs are about the sun, moon, and stars, and songs about magical transformations abound. In songs about orphans, the moon is often asked to become the orphan's father and the sun to become the mother. A dead father sometimes reappears transformed into an oak tree. There are songs for dances and games, humorous and satirical songs, and songs about family life. Other songs are about Lithuanian history and social commentary and protest.

MOVIES

A popular way of spending an evening is to watch a film at the local movie theater, found in many Lithuanian towns. Some of the movies are dubbed in Lithuanian, while others are shown in the original language with Lithuanian subtitles. Major US and European productions are usually shown. There is

Young musicians play on Street Music Day, a popular event in Vilnius, on May 21, 2016.

TENDING THE GARDEN

Lithuanians like growing things—vegetables in their backyards, and flowers and herbs on their balconies and windowsills. They are never more than a few generations from their farmer roots, and almost all maintain some kind of tie to the land. Most urban people own garden plots on the outskirts of the cities and towns. Restrictions limiting buildings on these plots have become unenforceable, and summer houses have become more and more substantial. About 14 percent of state land is used for garden plots by urban dwellers and educational establishments. In spring, summer, and early fall, families or groups of friends go to the plots on weekends to tend the gardens and fruit trees or just to relax. Older people who no longer have to worry about jobs just move out to their place for the summer.

also a small local movie industry; however, new film projects have been few due to a lack of funds. Well-known American film directors Jonas Mekas and Robert Zemeckis are both of Lithuanian descent.

SPORTS

The most favored individual sports are noncompetitive. Swimming is extremely popular, especially in rivers and lakes. Beach resorts are also well liked, especially the one at Palanga.

Fishing is a favorite pastime, too, and there are abundant fish in the thousands of lakes and rivers of Lithuania. When the lakes are frozen solid, ice fishing is practiced. A well-known spot for ice fishing is the Curonian Lagoon. Hang gliding is common in the town of Prienai, where gliders are produced. Ice skating, skiing, and tobogganing have long been popular among young Lithuanians too.

Competitive sports are basketball, volleyball, and soccer. Hands down, the most popular is basketball. During the Soviet era, Lithuania provided the best players for the Soviet team, and the Kaunas team won the Soviet championship twice. The basketball team took home the gold in the Europe Championship (now called EuroBasket) in 1937, 1939, and 2003. In 1992,

1996, and 2000, the national team won the bronze medal at the Summer Olympics, and came in fourth in 2004. In 2010, the team earned a bronze at the FIBA World Championship and five EuroBasket medals.

Every Lithuanian boy's hero is the great player Arvydas Sabonis, who played for the Portland Trail Blazers in the United States from 1995 to 2003. His son, Domantas Sabonis, also became an NBA player when he joined the Oklahoma City Thunder in 2016.

Many Lithuanians are also regular participants in activities organized by sports clubs. There are more than eight hundred sports clubs, including ones for weightlifting, wrestling, judo, and tennis. Young people particularly enjoy cycling and badminton.

HIKING AND FORAGING

Hikers of all ages walk throughout Lithuania, visiting historical and religious sites. Battle sites are particularly popular. At these areas, people often stop to learn folk and patriotic songs.

Arvydas Sabonis of the Portland Trail Blazers pauses during a game in 1999.

During the summer, Lithuanians travel over their picturesque country by bike, foot, and car, and on the waterways by canoe, raft, and boat. Along the way they visit history and craft museums, towns, cities, settlements, and farmsteads, national parks, ancient places of worship, forests, hills, and lakes. Birders often frequent the west coast, in particular the town of Vente to the east of the Curonian Lagoon, where large numbers of birds may be seen. Huge boulders are another attraction. One boulder is 75 feet (23 m) long, 21 feet (6.5 m) wide, and 13 feet (4 m) high.

Lithuanians are also fond of picking mushrooms in the forests, where there are more than one hundred varieties of edible mushrooms. People also go foraging during the summer and fall for wild strawberries, blueberries, raspberries, lingonberries, and cranberries.

STEPONAS DARIUS

The history of basketball in Lithuania begins with one of the country's great heroes, Steponas Darius. He was born in 1896. In 1907 his family emigrated to the United States, where he excelled at baseball, football, and basketball. He fought in France during World War I and returned to the United States with two decorations.

In 1920 he was one of the US volunteers who took part in the liberation of occupied Lithuania. He stayed in Lithuania for seven years. During that time, he introduced basketball to the country and became a champion sportsman.

After his return to the United States in 1927, he worked in civil aviation and founded a Lithuanian flying club, Vytis. Five years later, he and his colleague Stasys Girėnas set out to bring fame and glory to their newly independent nation by embarking on an epic flight from New York to Lithuania. They scraped together enough money to buy an old plane, which they called the Lituanica.

The plane took off from New York on July 15, 1933, and flew across the Atlantic in 37 hours 11 minutes, but it never arrived in Lithuania. No one knows why, but the plane crashed in Germany. Rumors that the Lituanica *had been deliberately brought down by the Germans did not improve international relations. Their bodies were taken to Kaunas, then the provisional capital, where sixty thousand people attended the funeral.*

Despite its tragic end, many felt that the flight had put Lithuania on the map. The duo's portraits appeared on postage stamps, coins, and medals, and numerous streets, bridges, and schools were named after them. In 2001 the pair was honored with a portrait on the 10 litas banknote.

Monuments have been erected in their memory in Chicago, Lithuania, and Poland. One of the most popular monuments to the heroes is near Anykščiai on a huge boulder called Puntukas. This ancient landmark is one of the country's mythical stones. In 1943, a Lithuanian sculptor was in the countryside, hiding from the Germans, and he made a shelter beside the boulder. To while away the time, he carved a relief of the faces of the two pilots into the stone, adding the text of their will, which had been written before they embarked on their historic flight.

SAUNAS AND ICE BATHS

Enjoying saunas is a popular leisure activity. Lithuanians love the alternate hot and cold sensations that a sauna and their country's climate provide. Saunas are built near streams or lakes, so that after a session in a steamy sauna, a bather can plunge into the icy waters next to it.

In the wintertime, a large number of Lithuanians take dips in "ice holes." Some even bravely swim in the Baltic Sea among the ice floes.

The town of Druskininkai, on the Nemunas River, is famous for its mineral springs and therapeutic mud, well-equipped sanatoriums, comfortable holiday homes, parks, beautiful surroundings, and pleasant climate. This health resort, situated 87 miles (140 km) from Vilnius, attracts some four hundred thousand visitors a year.

CLAY WHISTLES AND BIRDHOUSES

Clay whistles are popular, and adults make them for their children in an astonishing array of shapes and forms. Lithuanian children are particularly fond of clay whistles made in the shapes of horses, riders, and lambs for the boys, and ducklings, birds, and flowers for the girls.

In springtime, young and old alike occupy themselves making birdhouses. These are mounted on poles near homes to welcome the returning summer visitors—jackdaws, starlings, and others. Old wagon wheels are put on roofs or on tall trees to attract the returning storks looking for building sites for their sturdy nests.

Handmade clay whistles are charming folk art toys.

INTERNET LINKS

http://www.snowarena.lt
This is the English language site of Lithuania's Snow Arena in Druskininkai.

http://www.truelithuania.com/topics/lifestyle-in-lithuania/sports-in-lithuania
This site provides an excellent overview of basketball and other sports in Lithuania.

FESTIVALS

Traditional handcrafted Lithuanian Easter eggs fill a basket at a folk arts fair.

12

LIKE OTHER EUROPEAN COUNTRIES, Lithuania's annual holiday calendar includes national historical observances, religious traditions, and secular festivities—some with a nod to the country's pre-Christian pagan heritage. Strong family ties and the commitment of country people kept the spirit and memory of Lithuanian traditions alive through the Soviet years. Today, religious and seasonal festivals, as well as ethnic folk culture events, are publically celebrated all over Lithuania. Hundreds of youth and adult folkloric groups, including student ensembles from secondary schools to universities, often perform at these popular events.

Nesting storks are thought to bring good luck. To that end, Lithuanians celebrate Stork Day on March 25 with various old rituals. Farmers stir seeds to increase their germinating power. People bury dead snakes under their doorsteps, light straw fires, and watch for the return of the majestic white birds. Children find sweets and other little gifts, allegedly from the storks, hanging on tree branches and fences.

LITHUANIAN HOLIDAYS

January 1*	New Year's Day
January 6	Three Kings' Day
January 13	Defenders of Freedom Day: commemorates the victims of Soviet troops on January 13, 1991
February or March	Užgavėnės (Carnival)
February 16*	Independence Day (1918)
March 4	Saint Casimir's Day: celebrates the coming of spring
March 11	The Day of Restitution: independence from the Soviet Union in 1990
March/April*	Easter
June 14	Day of Mourning and Hope: commemorates the mass deportation of Lithuanians to Siberia in 1941
June 24	Midsummer (Saint Jonas Day or Dew Holiday)
July 6*	Statehood Day: coronation of Mindaugas in 1253
August 15	Feast of the Assumption
August 23	Black Ribbon Day: remembrance for victims of Stalinism and Nazism
September 8	Nation Day: birth of the Virgin Mary and the coronation of Vytautas the Great in 1430
November 1*	All Saints' Day
November 23	Lithuanian Soldiers' Day
December 24, 25*	Christmas Eve and Christmas Day

*Official public holidays

MIDSUMMER DAY

Saint Jonas' Day falls on June 24, which is Midsummer Day, or Rasos (Dew Holiday), in the pre-Christian tradition. When Catholicism arrived in Lithuania, the Church incorporated this major holiday into Christian activities by combining it with the popular saint's day, but many ancient traditions still predominate in modern celebrations of midsummer.

Most of the festivities take place on the eve of the holiday. Girls and women gather flowers and herbs, which are believed to heal illnesses if collected at this time. These are woven into wreaths and either worn on the head or cast adrift in streams and rivers. People light bonfires and sing and dance around them, jump over them, and play games. The glow from the bonfires can be seen from afar, spreading light over crops, thus ensuring protection from harm. The flames are believed to have cleansing and healing powers. Weeds from the fields are pulled up and thrown into the fires. Later, the ashes are spread on the fields. At home the hearth fire is extinguished and then rekindled with embers from the bonfire.

Women wear flowers for the Saint Jonas, or Dew Holiday, Festival in Klaipėda on June 24.

HARVEST FESTIVALS

Ancient Lithuanians' celebrations fell on the most significant days of the year: the solstices, equinoxes, and harvests. Since Lithuania is primarily an agricultural nation, it is not surprising that many festivals are connected with farming and animal husbandry.

There are many traditional festivities associated with the rye harvest. When the rye harvest begins, the first plants gathered are tied into a small sheaf. This bundle is called the *Diedas* (old man) or the Guest, and is set up behind the table in the place of honor. It stands there as a symbol of plenty.

Before the main harvest, the family gathers with neighboring families at the far end of their fields to divide a loaf of rye bread together, saying, "Bread meets bread" as they eat it.

The reapers leave a small patch of rye stalks growing on the field at the end of the harvest. When they have finished, they stand in a circle around this clump, cover their hands with scarves or aprons, and uproot any weeds from between the stalks. These stalks are then braided and bent toward the farmstead to ensure that wealth flows from the fields to the household.

The reapers weave a harvest wreath from the best ears of rye for the head harvester to carry to the owner of the farm. The entire group of harvesters greets the landowner, who then serves everyone a lavish harvest feast.

ALL SAINTS' DAY

All Saints' Day, celebrated on November 1, is an occasion to remember and pray for the dead. On this day, as well as on November 2, All Souls' Day, Lithuanians decorate family graves with flowers, plants, and burning candles. It is thought that doing this brings the spirits nearer and helps to form a bond between the living and the dead. Since ancient times, Lithuanians have believed that after death the soul separates from the body but continues existing among the living. In some places, bread is baked and distributed to the poor. This ensures that the coming year's honey and rye harvests will be plentiful.

CHRISTMAS

Lithuanians celebrate Christmas Eve, or Kūčios (KOO-chi-ohs), faithfully. The women scrub and decorate the house. In rural areas, the men clean the yard and prepare special fodder for the animals. When the day's work is done, everyone bathes and dresses in their best clothes. When the evening star

appears, the family sits down at the table. It is important to be at home for the Christmas Eve dinner, and sometimes people will undertake long journeys to be with their families. Travelers and friends are also welcomed.

For the evening meal the table is spread with hay in memory of the birth of Christ in the manger, and covered with a white linen cloth. Plates are decorated with a fir twig or sprig of myrtle. Sometimes hay is placed under or on each plate. A Christmas Eve wafer is placed on each plate. These wafers, *kaledaiciai* (kah-le-DY-chi-eye) are made of unleavened wheat dough, and blessed in the church. A cross is placed at the center of the table. People sit down at the table in order of seniority, leaving empty spaces for absent members.

The meal begins with a prayer. Then the head of the family breaks a wafer and shares it with all at the table, extending greetings and good wishes. Everyone else then does the same.

Customarily, twelve courses are placed on the table, one for each month of the year, signifying that the family will have enough food all year. The dishes are prepared from wheat, oat, and barley flours, groats (crushed grain

Christmas greetings and a whimsical Christmas tree light up the December evening in Vilnius.

of various cereals), fish, mushrooms, poppy seeds, fruits, berries, honey, and hemp oil. No milk or meat is served. The meal ends with a prayer and the singing of a Christmas hymn. After the feast, both adults and children enjoy telling fortunes by drawing stalks of hay from under the tablecloth. If a girl draws a thin stalk, for example, her future husband will be tall and thin. Or if a married man pulls a plump stem, it means a prosperous year for him. On farms the hay from the table is then given to the animals.

The Christmas tree tradition came to Lithuania at the beginning of the twentieth century. In 1908, pine trees were decorated on some farms in Zemaitija for the children of the laborers. In 1910 they appeared in a few schools and orphanages. After World War I the custom spread to the cities, but it took longer to reach the villages. The trees are decorated with ornaments made of straw, painted eggshells, and figures made out of pastry. These could be birds, horses, squirrels, lambs, moons, suns, stars, flowers, or other figurines. The tradition of Santa Claus or the Old Man of Christmas giving presents to children also started about this time.

Christmas Day is considered sacred and is celebrated more quietly. People sing hymns and carols and visit each other to exchange greetings.

SHROVETIDE

Shrovetide, or Užgavenes (OO-zhe-GAH-veh-nes), is celebrated in March on Shrove Tuesday, the last day before the forty-day fast for Lent that is traditional for Catholics. The verb *užgavèti* (OO-zhe-GAH-veh-tee) means "to eat well and heartily." This festival is full of humor, jokes, superstitions, fortune-telling, and feasting to celebrate the end of winter. It is a merry carnival, a masquerade full of pranks, with a drama performed outdoors to cast off winter and welcome spring. Elsewhere this is known as Mardi Gras or Carnival.

At dusk, men dress up in costumes with humorous, satirical, or animal masks. They go from house to house, deriding housewives or workers lagging behind in their chores. Some dress as evil spirits or demons with pitchforks. Many people dress up as traditional characters. Popular characters are Kanapinis, the Hemp Man, because during Lent hemp oil is used for light

MARGUCIAI, LITHUANIAN EASTER EGGS

Decorating Easter eggs is an ancient folk art practiced throughout Eastern Europe. In Lithuania, the eggs, called *margučiai*, are crafted with intricate designs in a wide variety of rich colors. The eggs are bathed in dyes made of natural materials, such as leaves, flowers, and vegetables. Decorations are applied using either of two methods. Designs

may be scratched on the eggshell's surface using a sharp, pointed object—this leaves a thin white line visible on the dyed shell. Alternatively, the eggs can be decorated with a wax-resist method. The artist carefully draws on the eggshell with hot wax. The cooled

wax then hardens in place and resists the subsequent dye. After several rounds of waxing and dyeing the egg, the crafter melts all the wax off the eggshell, revealing a colorful pattern or image.

In olden times, people thought the decorated eggs had mystical powers, and people gave them as gifts. Today, the finely crafted eggs still make for much-appreciated gifts, as beautiful and symbolic works of folk art.

instead of tallow candles; a thief looking for something to steal; a beggar; or characters rarely seen in the village—the doctor and the soldier. Animal figures include horses, goats, and storks. Men disguise themselves as women and vice versa. An old woman, More—a symbol of the clash between winter and spring—is wheeled about in a cart. In one hand she holds a flail and in the other a broom, for she cannot make up her mind whether she should continue to flail last year's harvest or start sweeping the yard and set about the spring cleaning!

PALM SUNDAY AND EASTER

It is traditional to attend church on Palm Sunday morning with a bunch of juniper or pussy willow branches. At first light on Palm Sunday, family members compete to get up before the others so that the early ones can tap the sleepers with the green branches, singing: "It is not me who is flogging you, it is the Palm Sunday juniper doing it. Easter comes in a week. Do you promise me an Easter egg?" After the church service, the pretend flogging continues in the streets. This is a way of wishing each other to be as healthy as the green twigs.

On Easter morning, the floggers receive decorated Easter eggs. The hard-cooked eggs are covered with wax designs then dipped in dyes, or first given a color bath and then carved with a sharp knife or a piece of glass. The eggs are eaten on Easter morning. Children receive their eggs from the Easter Granny, who leaves eggs in a tidy nest outside the house or in a basket hanging from a tree. The children never see her, of course, for she arrives before sunrise in a little cart pulled by a wax horse (the wax horse would melt if she came after the sun had risen).

FOLK MUSIC FESTIVALS

The best folk music performers are concentrated in Vilnius. Among the many folk music festivals held there, *Skamba skamba kankliai* (skahm-ba skahm-ba kan-kli-eye), held in the last week of May, is the most popular.

The largest folk singing festival is the Baltica Festival, held in a different Baltic city every year. The festival brings together singers and spectators from the three Baltic states and sometimes from Scandinavia as well. At the Baltica Festival in 1987, the flags of Lithuania, Latvia, and Estonia were displayed together for the first time since the Soviet occupation.

INTERNET LINKS

http://goeasteurope.about.com/od/lithuaniatravel/a/Lithuanias-Holidays.htm
Lithuania's main holidays are covered on this site, with special emphasis on Christmas traditions.

http://www.lithaz.org/arts/eggs/lit/methods.html
This site presents the myths and symbolism of Lithuanian Easter eggs along with some lovely photos.

http://lithuanianmha.org/holiday-traditions/velykos
This Lithuanian American site gives a good overview of Easter arts and customs, including a video.

http://ssk.lt/en
The home site of the Skamba Skamba Kankliai Festival, in English, includes many colorful photos.

FOOD

A cook presents platters of traditional foods at a folk arts festival in Vilnius.

13

THE CUSTOMARY FOODS OF Lithuania are based on the crops that grow best in the region's cool, moist, northern climate. Potatoes, beets, cabbages, mushrooms, and berries are everyday fare, as are barley and rye. Pork is the most common meat. Lithuanian cookery is somewhat heavy and straightforward—a homey fare that reflects the influence of German and Polish cooking. Tatar, Russian, and Belorussian tastes are also seen in the use of mild spices. Typical seasonings are caraway, garlic, onion, parsley, parsnip, dill, coriander, celery root, mustard, horseradish, fennel, and lovage (an herb of the carrot family).

Dishes vary in Lithuania according to the season. Animals are usually slaughtered in the fall and winter, so more meat is eaten at those times. During spring and summer, people consume more milk, vegetables, berries, mushrooms, and flour-based dishes. Fish from rivers, lakes, and the sea is abundant. The country's natural resources are well used, and there has always been an abundant supply of good food.

Stuffed potato dumplings called *cepelinai* are often said to be Lithuania's national dish. The oval-shaped dumplings are named after the zepplin, or airship, first manufactured in 1900 by the German Count Ferdinand von Zeppelin.

RYE BREAD

Lithuanians are very fond of dense bread made from dark rye flour, and they eat it at every meal. White bread is baked only on special occasions. Bakers bake large oblong loaves, covered with maple, cabbage, or other leaves to add flavor. The baker will often make a sign of the cross as a blessing over the first loaf in a batch, and make an impression of a cross into the last one.

At home, baking day is considered to be a special occasion, during which homes are quiet and no one argues for fear that the bread won't rise. If visitors arrive on baking day, they cannot leave until the baking is done so they can take a warm loaf home with them.

There are many superstitions associated with bread. A loaf of bread is inserted into the foundations of a new house to ensure that the family never runs out of bread. Farmers always plow a piece of bread into the first furrow in spring. The farmer's wife places a piece of bread under the first sheaf of rye during harvest time. When moving into a new house, a loaf of bread is

A loaf of traditional Lithuanian brown bread is decorated with a wreath of rye.

carried into the house along with pictures of saints. The bread, covered with a towel, is always placed in a special place in the house. Newlyweds are greeted with loaves of bread at the threshold of homes they may visit. A bride always takes a loaf of bread and some leaven (yeast or fermented dough) from her mother's mixture to her husband's home as a starter for her own bread. Important visitors are greeted with a loaf of bread on a towel. Slicing bread is always the proper task of the head of the family.

White curd cheese with caraway seeds is a favorite soft cheese.

MILK AND CHEESE

The dairy industry is very important in the Baltic states. Both fresh and sour milk are used in Lithuania. Milk is drunk sweet or curdled. Butter and fresh cheese are part of the everyday diet. Lithuanians make lots of soft and hard cheeses and a kind of cottage cheese called sweet cheese. This is made by boiling milk mixed with sugar and eggs, then adding a little curd into the boiling milk, thereby curdling all the milk. The curds are strained and caraway seeds are sometimes added for flavor. The mixture is then pressed into cheese.

Cheese is served with coffee on special occasions and at festive events. A special, dense, yellow cheese is made for the midsummer festival. Cheese is always served with buttered bread. It is also given as a present when visiting friends and relatives.

THE MANY USES OF THE POTATO

Potatoes were introduced into Lithuania in the eighteenth century and very soon became the most popular item on the Lithuanian plate. Lithuanians especially love boiled white potatoes served with sour or fresh milk.

A cepelinai, or zepplin-shaped potato dumpling.

Potatoes are used in soups, dumplings, porridge, pancakes, and savory puddings called *kugelis*. Grated potatoes are used to make sausages. A typical Lithuanian dish is boiled potatoes served with pounded and fried hemp seeds.

Each housewife has her favorite potato recipe. Potato pie is served with sour milk, cottage cheese, sour cream, and fried cubed bacon. Since the beginning of the twentieth century, *cepelinai*, or zeppelins—potato dumplings stuffed with meat and onions, mushrooms, or cheese—have become a favorite Lithuanian dish.

OTHER DISHES

The Lithuanian diet has become fairly uniform throughout the country, although certain dishes predominate in different regions. Zemaitians are still fond of all kinds of porridge and *kastinis* (KAH-sti-nis), a kind of butter. Dzukians specialize in buckwheat and mushroom dishes. Suvalkians delight in *skilandis* (ski-LAHN-dis), smoked pig's stomach or bladder filled with minced meat and seasoned with pepper, garlic, and sweet cottage cheese. Aukstaitians love their special large pancakes for breakfast.

Meat comes mostly from cattle, sheep, goats, and pigs, and less from fowl. Pork is the most common meat in the Lithuanian diet. Virtually every part of the pig is eaten, including the foot and the ear. Lean pork and bacon is boiled or baked. Meat is salted or smoked for longer storage. Freshwater fish is an important food source for those residing near rivers and lakes, while those along the seacoast enjoy many saltwater fish. Smoked fish is often sold at wayside stalls as a tasty form of fast food, while smoked eel is a special treat among the people of the Baltic coast. Eels are found in Kursiu Marios and some rivers and lakes, and they grow to be 4 feet (1.2 m) long and up to 9 pounds (4.1 kg) in weight.

Beets, cabbages, and turnips have long been a part of Lithuanian cuisine. Beet greens and roots are eaten freshly boiled or pickled, or used in soups. Cold beet soup, with sour milk, cucumbers, dill, and hard-cooked eggs is a popular dish in the hot summer months. Lithuania also has its own version of the hot Russian borscht, where mushrooms are added to the beet soup, and it is sometimes accompanied by rissoles (fried fish or meat cakes). Fresh or pickled cabbage soup is a common dish. Some twenty species of mushroom are eaten in Lithuania. They are used to flavor soups, especially beet soup, during Lent. A cream soup with vegetables, such as potatoes, peas, carrots, or cabbage, cooked with flour-dough dumplings or pasta, is frequently eaten for dinner.

Lithuanians enjoy a wide variety of mushrooms.

DRINKS

Milk is the most commonly consumed beverage. Coffee is by far the most popular hot drink, with tea a distant second. Both coffee and tea are served without milk.

Beer is the most popular alcoholic drink. Lithuanians started brewing beer in the sixteenth century. Today each of Lithuania's cities has its own brewery. Lithuanian beer is of high quality and is brewed stronger and sweeter than those found in Western Europe. Homemade beer is still brewed in some districts.

The head of the household begins a special meal by pouring a mug of beer from a pitcher and saying to the guests, "To your health. Drink, brothers, and celebrate!" He then spills a few drops, drinks the cup dry, fills it again and

hands it to a guest. The gathered people reply, "Be healthy" and "To your health." In this fashion, the cup makes it way down the table.

Sweet commercial soft drinks are widely available. Lithuania's most distinctive beverage is *gira* (GEE-rah), a slightly alcoholic soft drink made from either rye bread or caraway seeds. Birch sap flavored with black-currant leaves is also popular as a drink.

Midus (MI-doos), or mead, is a wine made from honey, often with herbs and other natural flavorings added. The ancient drink is produced commercially today, although the original recipe has been lost. Lithuania also produces several types of liqueurs as well as vodka and champagne.

KITCHENS

In old country houses, woodstoves are still used (with a gas or electric stove as a standby). Fuel is the dry branches and chopped wood of fallen trees gathered from the forest. The stoves also keep the houses warm.

Homes always contain a cellar, even in high-rise buildings in cities. In the countryside, cellars are dug outside and covered with an earth mound. Winter provisions are kept in the cellars: potatoes, beets, carrots, cabbages, onions, pumpkins, squashes, apples, sauerkraut, pickled cucumbers, and dried mushrooms. Most housewives preserve fruit and berries picked from the garden or forest. These, too, are stored in the cellar.

In Lithuanian kitchens, a clay pot is used as a double boiler for making soups and zeppelins, and a potato grater (electric or hand-turned) is indispensable because meals made with grated potatoes are an everyday affair.

Each family member has an assigned place at the table. The head of the household sits at the end by the wall in the place of honor. Traditionally, men sit on one side of the table with the women opposite them. Important guests are seated in the place of honor or beside it.

Should a visitor arrive unexpectedly while the family is at the table, the visitor greets the family with "Skanaus" (SKA-na-oos), or "Bon appétit." If the father returns the greeting with "You are welcomed," the guest is invited to join them at the table. Should the returned greeting simply be "Thank you," however, the guest is not welcomed at the table. This is rare, though, as guests, travelers, or even beggars who arrive at mealtime are always invited to the table.

Meals always begin with the slicing of bread by the head of the household. The first slice, the heel, is passed to the eldest son. The passing of bread continues down the table until each member of the family has taken a slice of bread from the father's hand. The remaining unsliced bread stays on the table. Old customs say the cut end of the bread should face the most important corner of the house. Alternatively, it could also be placed facing the sun. Placing the loaf upside down on the table must never be done as it is believed that act foretells that death will come to the household. Neither should the cut end of the bread face the door, or madness will afflict the women and they will leave the home. Slices of bread are always broken with two hands because making the bread requires two hands.

Lithuanians pride themselves on their hospitality and will relentlessly urge visitors to eat a little more. No one, even guests, leave the table until everyone has finished eating.

INTERNET LINKS

http://www.cooks.com/rec/search/0,1-0,lithuanian,FF.html
This recipe site includes many reader-submitted Lithuanian dishes.

https://delishably.com/vegetable-dishes/traditional-lithuanian-dishes
This food site gives a good overview of traditional foods, with pictures, but no recipes.

SALTIBARSCIAI (COLD BEET SOUP)

This refreshing, vivid pink soup is often served in the summertime.

1 pound (450 grams) unpeeled red beets, stem trimmed (amount is approximate)
2 medium cucumbers, peeled, seeded and cut into ½-inch (1.25 cm) pieces
2 green onions, trimmed and sliced
2 peeled, hard-cooked eggs
1 cup (250 millilitres) sour cream
4 cups (1 liter) buttermilk or plain kefir
Fresh dill, chopped
Fresh chives, chopped
Salt to taste

Cover the whole beets in water and boil in a covered saucepan over medium heat until tender.

While the beets are cooking, chop the egg whites finely. Mash the egg yolks with ¼ teaspoon (1.23 mL) salt and combine with sliced green onion, and reserve.

When beets are cooked, reserve the cooking liquid and set aside. Let the beets cool, and then carefully peel off the skins. (Juices will stain skin and clothing.) Grate the beets coarsely.

Strain beet cooking liquid and return it to the cooking pot. Add buttermilk and sour cream, blending well. Mix in the grated beets, chopped cucumbers, chopped egg whites, and yolk-onion mixture. Stir until well blended.

Pour into a container and refrigerate until well chilled. Adjust seasonings, if necessary, and serve with chopped dill. Adjust seasonings. This soup is often served with a warm, peeled, boiled potato on the side.

KUGELIS (POTATO PUDDING)

1 tablespoon (15 mL) butter
4 large russet potatoes
½ pound (230 g) bacon
1 medium onion, finely chopped
4 eggs, beaten
½ cup (250 mL) milk
Kosher salt and cracked black pepper

Preheat the oven to 400 degrees Fahrenheit (200 degrees Celsius). Butter an 8 x 8 inch (20 x 20 centimeter) baking pan. Grate the potatoes on the large holes of a box grater, and place the grated potatoes in a bowl of cold water.

Cook the bacon over medium high heat until it is crisp and the fat is rendered, about 7 minutes. Remove the bacon and drain on paper towels. Once it is cool enough to handle, coarsely chop the bacon. Pour off all but 2 tablespoons (30 mL) of bacon fat, return the pan to medium heat, and add the chopped onion. Cook until onions are soft and brown, about 10 minutes. Remove from heat and reserve.

Combine beaten eggs and milk and season with salt and pepper. Drain the grated potatoes by placing them in a clean dishtowel—a few handfuls at a time—folding the towel over the potatoes, and twisting the towel ends firmly, over the sink, to wring out the excess water. Add the drained potatoes to egg/milk mixture and repeat with remaining potatoes. Add the chopped bacon and onions to the potato mixture and, using a wooden spoon, mix until all ingredients are well combined. Pour into prepared baking pan. Place in preheated oven and bake until potatoes are soft and brown and beginning to crisp, about 1 hour. Serve with sour cream and apple sauce.

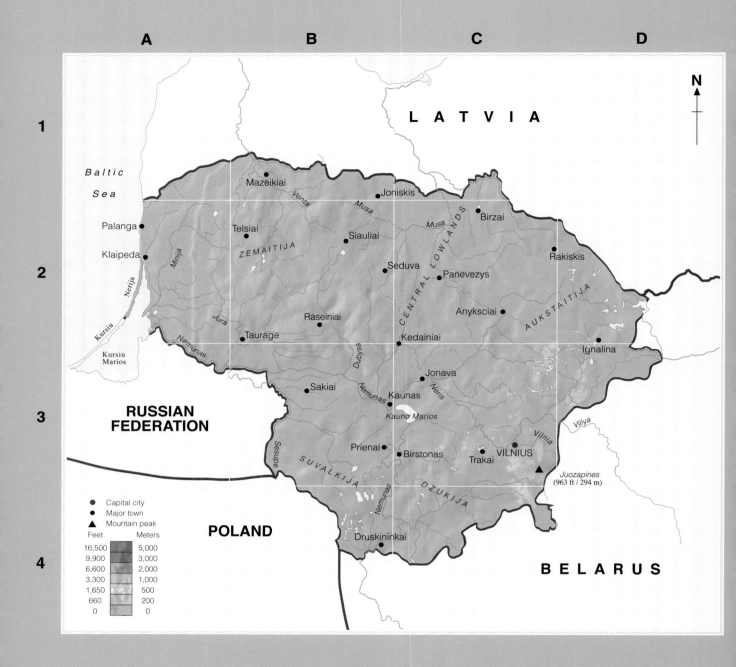

A   B   C   D

N

1

L A T V I A

Baltic Sea

2

Palanga

Klaipeda

Nerija

Kursiu

Kursiu Marios

RUSSIAN FEDERATION

3

Minija

Z E M A I T I J A

Mazeikiai

Joniskis

Venta

Musa

Telsiai

Siauliai

Seduva

Musa

Birzai

Rakiskis

C E N T R A L L O W L A N D S

Panevezys

Anyksciai

A U K S T A I T I J A

Ignalina

Jura

Raseiniai

Nemunas

Taurage

Dubysa

Kedainiai

Sakiai

Nemunas

Jonava

Neris

Kaunas

Kauno Marios

Vilnia

Viliya

Sesupe

Prienai

Birstonas

Trakai

VILNIUS

*Juozapines
(963 ft / 294 m)*

S U V A L K I J A

Nemunas

D Z U K I J A

POLAND

Druskininkai

4

B E L A R U S

● Capital city
● Major town
▲ Mountain peak

Feet	Meters
16,500	5,000
9,900	3,000
6,600	2,000
3,300	1,000
1,650	500
660	200
0	0

MAP OF LITHUANIA

ECONOMIC LITHUANIA

Manufacturing

- Electronics
- Food Processing
- Furniture Making
- Petroleum Refinery
- Shipbuilding
- Textiles

Natural Resources

- Amber
- L Limestone
- Sand

Services

- Airport
- Seaport
- Tourism

Agriculture

- Cattle Farming
- Fishing
- Potatoes
- Sugar Beets
- Vegetables

ABOUT THE ECONOMY

OVERVIEW

The three former Soviet Baltic republics were severely hit by the 2008—2009 financial crisis, but Lithuania has rebounded and become one of the fastest growing economies in the EU. Lithuania's ongoing recovery hinges on export growth, which is being hampered by economic slowdowns in the EU and Russia. Lithuania joined the eurozone on January 1, 2015.
(All estimates from 2015 unless stated.)

GROSS DOMESTIC PRODUCT (GDP)

$41.27 billion (official exchange rate)

GDP GROWTH

1.6 percent

GDP BY SECTOR

agriculture: 3.2 percent
industry: 30.2 percent
services: 66.6 percent

CURRENCY

The Lithuanian *litas* (LTL) was the currency of Lithuania until January 2015, when it was replaced by the euro (EUR).
Banknotes: €5, €10, €20, €50, €100, €200, €500
Coins: 1 cent (c), 2c, 5c, 10c, 20c, 50c, €1, €2

$1 (USD) = €0.94 Euro (EUR) (November 2016)

WORKFORCE

1.47 million

UNEMPLOYMENT RATE

9.1 percent

INFLATION RATE

—0.7 percent

NATURAL RESOURCES

Peat, arable land, gravel, construction sand, quartz sand, dolomite, clay, limestone, brick clay, amber

AGRICULTURAL PRODUCTS

Grain, potatoes, sugar beets, flax, vegetables, beef, milk, eggs, fish, and pork

INDUSTRIES

Machinery, appliances, petroleum refining, shipbuilding, furniture, textiles, food processing, electronic components, computers, amber jewelry, information technology, video games, biotechnology

MAJOR EXPORTS

Refined fuel, machinery and equipment, chemicals, textiles, foodstuffs, plastics

MAJOR IMPORTS

Oil, natural gas, machinery and equipment, transport equipment, chemicals, textiles and clothing, metals

MAJOR TRADE PARTNERS

Russia, Germany, Poland, Latvia, Estonia

CULTURAL LITHUANIA

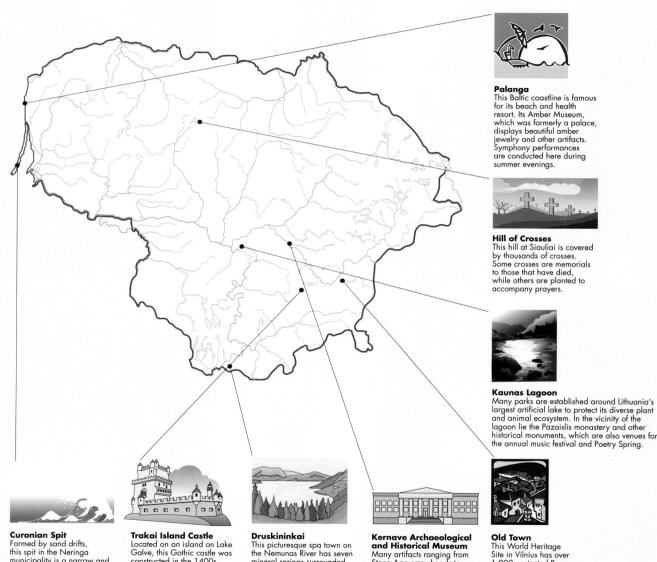

Palanga
This Baltic coastline is famous for its beach and health resort. Its Amber Museum, which was formerly a palace, displays beautiful amber jewelry and other artifacts. Symphony performances are conducted here during summer evenings.

Hill of Crosses
This hill at Siauliai is covered by thousands of crosses. Some crosses are memorials to those that have died, while others are planted to accompany prayers.

Kaunas Lagoon
Many parks are established around Lithuania's largest artificial lake to protect its diverse plant and animal ecosystem. In the vicinity of the lagoon lie the Pazaislis monastery and other historical monuments, which are also venues for the annual music festival and Poetry Spring.

Curonian Spit
Formed by sand drifts, this spit in the Neringa municipality is a narrow and isolated sandbar. Within the municipality lie four villages. Fishing and Jet Skiing are popular activities here.

Trakai Island Castle
Located on an island on Lake Galve, this Gothic castle was constructed in the 1400s. A moat separates the main tower from the courtyard where numerous concerts and plays are staged. The tower is also home to the Trakai History Museum.

Druskininkai
This picturesque spa town on the Nemunas River has seven mineral springs surrounded by natural forest reserves. The springs' high saline content is used in the treatment of nervous system disorders, among others. In 2003 Druskininkai was voted as one of the ten leading spa towns in Europe.

Kernave Archaeological and Historical Museum
Many artifacts ranging from Stone Age arrowheads to medieval jewelry are housed here. The museum is situated beside a neo-Gothic parish church. Every July, the Living Archaeology Days Festival is held in the village.

Old Town
This World Heritage Site in Vilnius has over 1,000 protected Baroque, Gothic, Renaissance, and Neoclassical monuments. The heart of the town, Pilies Street, has many street markets and cafés.

ABOUT THE CULTURE

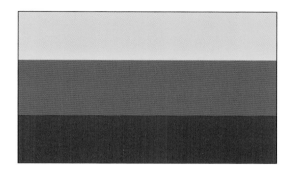

OFFICIAL NAME
Lietuvos Respublika (Republic of Lithuania)

FLAG DESCRIPTION
Three equal horizontal bands of yellow (topmost), green, and red.

TOTAL AREA
25,174 square miles (65,300 square km) of land

CAPITAL
Vilnius

POPULATION
2,854,235 (2016 estimate)

ETHNIC GROUPS
Lithuanian 84.1 percent, Polish 6.6 percent, Russian 5.8 percent, Belorussians 1.2 percent, others 1.1 percent (2011)

RELIGIOUS GROUPS
Roman Catholic 77.2 percent, Russian Orthodox 4.1 percent, Old Believer 0.8 percent, Evangelical Lutheran 0.6 percent, Evangelical Reformist 0.2 percent, other (including Sunni Muslim, Jewish, Greek Catholic, and Karaite) 0.8 percent, none 6.1 percent, unspecified 10.1 percent (2011)

BIRTH RATE
10 births / 1,000 Lithuanians (2016)

INFANT MORTALITY RATE
3.8 deaths / 1,000 live births (2016)

LIFE EXPECTANCY AT BIRTH
74.9 years
Male: 69.5 years
Female: 80.6 years (2016)

DEATH RATE
14.5 deaths / 1,000 Lithuanians (2016)

POPULATION GROWTH RATE
—1.06 percent (2016)

LANGUAGES
Lithuanian (official) 82 percent, Russian 8 percent, Polish 5.6 percent, other 0.9 percent, unspecified, 3.5 percent (2011)

LITERACY RATE
99.8 percent (2015)

LEADERS IN POLITICS
Chief of state: President Dalia Grybauskaite (since July 2009)
Head of government: Prime Minister Saulius Skvernelis (since November 2016)

TIMELINE

IN LITHUANIA	IN THE WORLD
2500 BCE Indo-European tribes settle along the Baltic shoreline of present-day Lithuania.	
	753 BCE Rome is founded.
100–900 CE The Lithuanians develop a prosperous trading empire with the Romans that covers northeastern Europe.	**116–117 CE** The Roman Empire reaches its greatest extent, under Emperor Trajan
	600 Height of the Mayan civilization
1000 The start of feudalism in the Baltic region. The Lithuanians, the largest tribe, emerge dominant.	**1000** The Chinese perfect gunpowder and begin to use it in warfare.
1236 – 1253 King Mindaugas unites the small feudal states of Lithuania into a duchy.	
1392 – 1430 Under Grand Duke Vytautas's rule, Lithuania becomes one of the largest states in Europe.	**1530** Beginning of transatlantic slave trade organized by the Portuguese in Africa.
1569 Lithuania and Poland form the Union of Lublin, sharing the same government.	**1620** Pilgrims sail the *Mayflower* to America.
	1776 US Declaration of Independence
1795 Lithuania is absorbed by Russia, and military uprisings against Russian rule begins.	**1789–1799** The French Revolution
1891 Russia imposes a press ban on books and papers printed in Lithuanian.	**1869** The Suez Canal is opened.
1915 German troops occupy Lithuania during World War I.	**1914–1919** World War I takes place.
1918 Lithuania proclaims independence.	
1941–1944 German army occupies Lithuania. The Nazis send Lithuanian Jews to death camps.	

IN LITHUANIA	IN THE WORLD
1944	**1939–1945**
The Soviet Union absorbs Lithuania into its Communist regime.	World War II occurs.
	1949
	The North Atlantic Treaty Organization (NATO) is formed.
	1969
1988	Apollo 11 lunar landing. Neil Armstrong
The Lithuanian Movement for Reconstruction (Sajudis) is established.	becomes first human to step on the moon.
1990	
Lithuanian Communist Party and Sajudis declare Lithuanian independence.	
1991	**1991**
Lithuania joins the United Nations.	Breakup of the Soviet Union.
1993	
The litas is reintroduced as national currency.	**2001**
	Terrorists crash planes in New York, Washington, D.C., and Pennsylvania.
	2003
2004	War in Iraq begins.
Lithuania joins NATO and the EU.	
2008	**2008**
Parliament bans display of Soviet and Nazi symbols.	US elects first African American president, Barack Obama.
	Economic crisis triggers global recession.
2009	
Independent Dalia Grybauskaite wins presidential election by a wide margin.	**2011**
	Syrian civil war begins, killing more than 250,000, displacing 11 million, and triggering refugee crisis.
	2014
2015	Islamic State (ISIS) takes control of large swaths of Syria and Iraq, proclaims creation of new caliphate.
Lithuania joins the eurozone, adopts euro as national currency in place of litas.	
2016	**2015–2016**
Saulius Skvernelis becomes prime minister of Lithuania.	ISIS attacks targets in Belgium and France.

GLOSSARY

birbynes (beer-BEE-nus)
A reed whistle

delmonas (dayl-MOH-nus)
A traditional decorative handbag

gira (GEE-rah)
A slightly alcoholic soft drink made from either rye bread or caraway seeds

glasnost
Openness; a Soviet reform policy of the 1980s

jonkelis (YONG-kay-lis)
A Lithuanian dance

kaledaiciai (kah-le-DY-chi-eye)
Christmas Eve wafers

kanklės (KAHN-klis)
A traditional stringed musical instrument

kastinis (KAH-sti-nis)
A kind of butter popular in Zemaitija

klumpes (KLOOM-pus)
Traditional wooden shoes

Kucios (KOO-chi-ohs)
Christmas Eve

lamždelis (lum-zhe-DAY-lis)
A wooden recorder

midus (MI-doos)
Mead, an ancient alcoholic drink made of honey

patarle (PAH-tehr-lay)
A proverb; a brief wise observation

perestroika
Restructuring; a Soviet reform policy of the 1980s

polytheism
The worshipping of many gods

raudos (RAO-dohs)
Laments or farewell songs

Sajudis (SAH-yoo-dis)
A political organization that advocated Lithuanian independence

salde (SAHL-day)
A soft drink cordial made from rye

Seimas (SAY-i-mahs)
The Lithuanian parliament

skilandis (ski-LAHN-dis)
A dish of smoked pig's stomach or bladder stuffed with seasoned meat

šustas (SHOOS-tahs)
A Lithuanian dance

Užgavenes (OO-zhe-GAH-veh-nes)
Shrovetide festival

Vytis (VEE-tis)
The charging white knight on a white horse that is the state emblem of Lithuania

žekelis (ZHAY-kay-lis)
A Lithuanian dance

zeppelin
A potato dumpling

FOR FURTHER INFORMATION

BOOKS

Belonogoff, Lara. *Lithuania—Culture Smart! The Essential Guide to Customs and Culture*. London: Kuperard, 2010.

Cassedy, Ellen. *We Are Here: Memories of the Lithuanian Holocaust*. Lincoln: University of Nebraska Press, 2012.

DK. *Eyewitness Travel Guide: Estonia, Latvia, and Lithuania*. New York: DK Publishing, 2015.

Gieysztor de Gorgey, Maria. *Art of Lithuanian Cooking*. New York: Hippocrene Books, 2001.

Gordon, Harry. *The Shadow of Death: The Holocaust in Lithuania*. Lexington: The University Press of Kentucky, 1992.

ONLINE

BBC News. Lithuania Country Profile. http://www.bbc.com/news/world-europe-17536867

Central Intelligence Agency. The World Factbook: Lithuania. https://www.cia.gov/library/publications/the-world-factbook/geos/lh.html

European Union: Lithuania. https://europa.eu/european-union/about-eu/countries/member-countries/lithuania_en

Lithuania Celebrates 100. http://www.lietuva.lt/100/en

Lithuania Online. http://www.online.lt/hgov

Lithuania: Real Is Beautiful. http://www.lithuania.travel/en-gb

Lonely Planet. Lithuania. https://www.lonelyplanet.com/lithuania

My Government: Gateway to the Government of the Republic of Lithuania. https://lrv.lt/en

FILMS

Algimantas Puipa. *Elze's Life*. Lietuvos Kino Studija, 1999.

Jonas Mekas. *Reminiscences of a Journey to Lithuania*. 1972.

Jonas Viatkus. *Utterly Alone*. Vilnius: V & K Holding, 2004.

MUSIC

Songs and Dances from Lithuania. Dainava, 2001.

Songs by Lithuanian Composers. Lyra Classics, 2003.

Vel: Lithuanian Chamber Music. Guild, 2005.

BIBLIOGRAPHY

BBC News. Lithuania country profile. January 22, 2016. http://www.bbc.com/news/world-europe-17536867

———Lithuania profile—Timeline. February 25, 2015. http://www.bbc.com/news/world-europe-17540745

Dunningham, Elizabeth. "Baltic Way Protest Remembered." Al Jazeera, August 25, 2009. http://www.aljazeera.com/news/europe/2009/08/200982414223654590.html

European Environment Agency. Lithuania. http://www.eea.europa.eu/soer-2015/countries/lithuania

Fein, Esther. "Baltic Citizens Link Hands to Demand Independence." *The New York Times*, August 24, 1989. http://www.nytimes.com/1989/08/24/world/baltic-citizens-link-hands-to-demand-independence.html

Heritage Foundation, The, and *The Wall Street Journal*. 2016 Index of Economic Freedom, Lithuania. http://www.heritage.org/index/country/lithuania

Jasaitis, Jonas, and Ingrid Karlsson. "Case Study Lithuania: A Rural Country in Transition." Baltic University. http://www.balticuniv.uu.se/index.php/component/docman/doc_download/1492-chapter-19-a-rural-country-in-transition-alternatives-for-lithuania

Knudsen, Ida Harboe. *New Lithuania in Old Hands: Effects and Outcomes of Europeanization in Rural Lithuania*. New York: Anthem Press, 2012.

Numbeo. Cost of Living in Lithuania. https://www.numbeo.com/cost-of-living/country_result.jsp?country=Lithuania

Reuters. "Lithuania power prices hit record low on imports from Sweden." February 23, 2016. http://af.reuters.com/article/commoditiesNews/idAFL8N1624IF

TrueLithuania.com. http://www.truelithuania.com

INDEX

INDEX